The Cambridge Code

The Cambridge Code

One Simple Test to Uncover
Who You Are

Dr Emma Loveridge and Dr Curly Moloney

bluebird
books for life

First published 2021 by Bluebird
an imprint of Pan Macmillan
The Smithson, 6 Briset Street, London EC1M 5NR
EU representative: Macmillan Publishers Ireland Limited,
Mallard Lodge, Lansdowne Village, Dublin 4
Associated companies throughout the world
www.panmacmillan.com

Hardback ISBN 978-1-5290-2563-7
Trade paperback ISBN 978-1-5290-3977-1

135798642

A CIP catalogue record for this book is available from the British Library.

Typeset in Minion by Jouve (UK), Milton Keynes
Printed and bound by CPI Group (UK) Ltd, Croydon, CR0 4YY

Visit www.panmacmillan.com to read more about all our books
and to buy them. You will also find features, author interviews and
news of any author events, and you can sign up for e-newsletters
so that you're always first to hear about our new releases.

Contents

Part One | The World Inside Our Mind

'The thing that we learn first stays with us longest, and
is the most difficult to unlearn.' (Anon.)

A child listens carefully as her father tries to explain to her that an iceberg is like a mountain, 'but you can only see the tip. The rest of it is hidden in the darkness under the sea. A mysterious darkness', he tells her, 'full of eerie light and amazing water-carved features in the ice and fish living in secret caves, waving their tails at the white whales. If you were the captain of a ship', he says, 'then you would need to seek out the mysterious world underneath the visible surface, or you wouldn't know how to steer the ship around the unseen dangers.' And he draws her a little picture of the iceberg, a line where the sea came, and a ship wrecked on the tip with the captain upside down and frowning. She frowns in her turn and says, 'I can see the mountain under the sea in the picture, so why can't the captain?' 'Ah', says her father, 'so much easier to look under another's swirling sea than the one we are in ourselves.' She got terribly frightened that her home was about to be overwhelmed by the deep, so literal is the imaginative world of a small child.

Much later, as an adult, she remembers this story and is immediately transported back to being that child, seeing her family floating away as dark blue water full of Beluga whales comes rising out of nowhere. She is considering how to rescue others in the house and her heartbeat is rising. She suddenly realises she is holding her breath in anticipation, even though she is several thousand miles from the nearest arctic waters.

As a metaphor for the subconscious, the iceberg is hard to beat. We each have a world inside us that, at times, operates independently of the present moment and, at other times, in conjunction with the present reality of the world around us. Who we are now has been formed by our childhood experiences. We all fleetingly 'slip' in and out of these unconscious worlds – how 'old' our mind makes us feel at any given moment on any given day depends on an infinite number of factors, past and present. We will often slip down into an early childhood experience, then climb – with some relief – back to our adult state of mind.

As you read this, maybe your mind was taken somewhere other than the present? Perhaps some experience crept up on you, a sense of the past within you, full of love or fear. Whatever your experience, the journey we have set out in this book is for you. It is a journey that we will travel together and, along the way, we will check in on how the foundations and scaffolding of your mind have been formed. You will learn to have considerable say over the invisible as well as the visible part of your mind, which will give you more power over the many different and often challenging parts of your life.

What The Cambridge Code Does:
Mapping the DNA of Your Mind

The Cambridge Code was developed to uncover subconscious potential that lies beyond the reach of established psychological measurement.

Like a DNA test for the mind, The Cambridge Code allows people to look beneath the surface at their own fundamental characteristics, giving an insight that isn't just about behaviour or thoughts but the deep subconscious pathways that make us who we are. Knowledge or even just an awareness about these characteristics gives us the power to make decisions in informed ways and choose what really suits us in life. It also enables us to understand why we are likely to behave in the ways that we do. Understanding our subconscious mind can help us unlock our potential in life and in work.

So often, our early experiences and impressions inspire interests that go on to shape our whole lives. For Dr Emma Loveridge, who went on to be the Clinical Director of the family clinic she founded, her father's iceberg story was the first spark in her desire to know more about our inner worlds. For Dr Curly Moloney, Loveridge's co-author and the inspiration behind the whole project, it was the study of medicine and behaviour that drove her. And yet they both came to the same conclusion: what if it were possible to lift the lid on your mind and not only see inside it, but understand its workings, too?

The brain as an organ is relatively easy to see – after all, we have brain surgeons – but the mind is a more complex feature; we do not have mind surgeons. The power of our minds – to imagine, learn, create, dream, think and choose – is, if we can make the subconscious work for us, our human superpower. It affects every single aspect of our lives: our relationships, our careers, our whole sense of happiness. It can work for us, or it can trip us up repeatedly, and sometimes we don't consciously understand why. The Cambridge Code is, quite simply, a way of imaging your subconscious mind, and making it work for you.

Imagine that you are having an overhaul of your health and you decide to consult with a heart specialist. She might arrange various investigations: blood tests, an ECG (electrocardiogram) to check your heart's rhythm, an echocardiogram to see its structure. She would use all the information to assess how your heart is functioning and to formulate advice on measures to improve things. She might, for example, suggest a change in diet, or more exercise, or a change in medication.

Imagine now that as part of this health overhaul you want to check out how your subconscious mind is faring. As we've said, there are no simple tests or scans here. One way to gain information would be to seek help from a psychotherapist. With their expertise, you may be able to delve deep below conscious thought to the unconscious depths. Down here lie the instincts and drivers that shape our thoughts, desires and choices. They may be deep-seated – and some will be positive while others are more difficult to accept – yet they are the things that make us who we are and it can be very enlightening to see them.

It has been estimated that between six and eight hours of work with a clinician would give you a reasonable 'image' of the mind. One of the difficulties for many of us is that it's hard to find the time and the funds for this kind of provision. Although The Cambridge Code is not the same as a face-to-face encounter, the ambition of this tool is to give a wider audience this kind of insight in approximately half an hour, in the privacy of your home or office.

It works like this: you take a test with about forty questions, which has been designed by a team of clinical scientists who have made use of well-recognised standard psychotherapeutic clinical models. It takes as its underlying premise the concept that the first eighteen years of our lives are formative: they shape the way we think and operate in adult life. The Code works by nudging our subconscious minds to consider various different scenarios, then examines how we would act and feel in those moments. The test can feel exciting, interesting, intrusive or challenging. Indeed, not unlike the experience of working with a therapist.

Your answers are passed through two sets of complex computerised algorithms, which have been developed over many years by scientists and psychotherapists. This produces a result of the profile of descriptors that make up your unique subconscious mind, which you will receive on-screen. It is equivalent to inputting a mass of jargon into one end of a modern-day decoding Enigma machine and receiving from the other end a read-out of the code. Only, in this case, it is your own individual mind code. The DNA of your mind.

Your results will be presented to you as an analysis of twelve fundamental areas of the mind, which we have represented visually as brain domains. Interpreting your results is a bit like looking at an ECG tracing or a laboratory blood test: you need guidance from the specialist in order to understand exactly what the bit of paper means for you. The online test will generate a brief report that you can use in conjunction with this book to understand your unique result profile. It does this in layman's terms, in an accessible way that will guide you to a deep understanding in minutes.

Understanding your Cambridge Code profile will give you insight into yourself and your innate preferences, risks and characteristics. It will enable you to understand what suits you in work and life and what does not; why you have a tendency to act, react, think and behave in certain ways in specific situations. It is like seeing your instincts written out for you. We have found that some people, on seeing their results, feel like they are looking at a version of themselves that they have known forever. Other people see things that they were definitely not expecting, and for them it can take a while for the results to really ring true.

While none of us can control our childhood experiences, we can control our responses to those experiences. We can begin to learn why we react in the way that we do to certain situations and why we make certain decisions. This book is not going to tell you how to fix things; its aim is to bring your subconscious tendencies and responses to your conscious attention, so that you can choose behaviour for yourself. Self-knowledge gives us choice, and that is the aim here. Once we know more about ourselves, we can steer our passage through life with more insight and control, making wiser choices, taking precautions in areas of vulnerability, and therefore hopefully making fewer mistakes. We can unlock potential in our relationships, our workplaces and our family environments to benefit our wellbeing overall.

Accessing Your Cambridge Code Profile

By purchasing this book, you have made the first step towards accessing your unconscious potential. We hope that you enjoy taking The Cambridge Code, find the results illuminating and embrace them as part of your journey towards a deeper understanding of the unique way in which your mind works.

This book also brings with it your free immediate online access to The Cambridge Code questionnaire. Whether you do this now or later is up to you. You may be impatient to go to the questionnaire and get your results profile straightaway, and feel that this will allow you to take the test in a more uninformed and unbiased manner. Then, when you read the rest of the book, you might be able to concentrate on those sections that appear more relevant to you. Alternatively, you may opt to read the book first and learn fully about the background to the different brain types so that, when you access your own profile, you will be forewarned and forearmed. There is no right or wrong way to approach The Cambridge Code; the choice is yours.

Whenever you are ready to take the questionnaire, use the link below to go to The Cambridge Code website. Scratch off the panel on the sticker on the inside back cover of this book to obtain your unique access code, then simply enter this in the box on the screen and follow the instructions to create an account and complete the online tool. You will get your results automatically when you finish the questionnaire. Click on the button to go to your report on-screen, and you will also be able to download a PDF if you wish. If you have any problems accessing the tool or your results, please get in touch with us through the website contact page.

www.thecambridgecode.com/redeem

The Cambridge Code in Practice

So how exactly does The Code work? We all recognise that we behave a little differently in different environments. For some of us, our behaviour varies at different times of the day, too: for example, many of us aren't really 'morning people'. However, the reality is that there are fundamental aspects of our personality that are deeply rooted within us that underlie our developmental axis and govern our potential for growth. These are the characteristics that sit deep within the workings of our mind, beneath the level of conscious thought and behaviour. These subconscious aspects affect everything we do, the way we approach and react to all the events and interactions of our lives. These are the essential parts of ourselves that are there first thing in the morning and still there when we go to bed at night. They are our core.

Psychologists believe that the more we understand about our core characteristics, the more we can recognise what really suits us and the more we will be able to flourish. When we are in a situation that doesn't really fit, a relationship or a job that is not really aligned with our core, the less 'whole' as a person we are likely to feel. Our wellbeing depends very much on our internal alignment with our external life.

The Cambridge Code cuts straight to the centre of our subconscious. As said earlier, it is the brainchild of Emma Loveridge and Curly Moloney, both Cambridge graduates, who over a period of time became determined to create a tool that would allow people to access their hidden subconscious depths. They each bring a very different perspective to the project. For Emma, it was a desire to broaden and deepen our understanding of the impact of the unconscious on our mental wellbeing. For Curly, with her background in corporate business, the aim was to create a swifter, more insightful psychometric assessment. Both spent many years researching and developing The Code, which is founded in well-established psychological and neuroscientific principles. With support from a team of Cambridge psychologists, and after many years of scientific research and rigorous trialling, The Cambridge Code was born. Since its beginnings in 2013, many thousands of people have used this Code, and benefited greatly from its insights.

The Model for The Cambridge Code:
Catching the Moment We Slip

Consider this scenario: a mature, highly experienced person arrives to give a talk to a large audience. As they arrive, they trip over the doorstep and fall. At this moment their state of mind changes from the 'competent adult' they started out as, and by the time they hit the floor they feel something very different. It could be a baby-like state, where they feel quite dependent and would really like someone to help them get up. Or it could be a toddler state, where they get themselves up without a hand because they feel the need to be independent. Then, rather than accepting it is their own fault for tripping up, they tell off the stair or the carpet. Or they could end up in the ten-year-old state of mind where they just need someone to say, 'Come on, up you get!'– i.e., an external authority to encourage them to keep going in life. Then again, they could arrive at the adolescent state of mind, where they are cripplingly embarrassed that they have made themselves look clumsy and foolish in front of people whom they respect and want to impress. Now they have been noticed, but in a negative way, and they just want the floor to open and swallow them up.

In this situation, every one of us would slip to a different state of mind. But what actually matters is not that we have fallen down this trajectory from adult through adolescent, child, toddler to baby, or even where we've landed. What matters is, *can we recover*? Some people can get up and continue on their way in a very adult manner – the recovery is immediate. Some need a cup of tea to quell their adrenaline and calm down. Others will have to go home – they cannot possibly carry on as normal now. And some will legislate against the institution that owns the step.

What this example shows us is that every single one of us, every day, goes up and down this developmental trajectory. Most of us don't even notice, it is just a part of daily life. We can be walking along and bump into a sibling, and immediately, unconsciously, our state of mind changes, reverting to a time when we were growing up together, with all its attendant rivalries and preoccupations.

Taking Our Steps up the Ladder:
The Developing States of Mind

Most of us are generally familiar with the concept that childhood physical development has well-defined stages: for example, sitting at six months, crawling at eight months, walking at eleven months, teething at a year. We understand that there will be variations in the trajectory: some children, for example, don't walk until they're eighteen months old.

But we may not realise that the trajectory of childhood *emotional* development is a similar pathway with similarly defined stages. Again, there will be variation from the usual trajectory: some children reach emotional milestones more slowly than others, for example, if they are over-protected by a parent. But nevertheless, there is broad general agreement on when the transitional times occur and how the stages are characterised. Infancy (0–2 years) is typified by maternal dependence; childhood (2–7 years) by a separation of identity from that of the carer; latency (7–10 years) by growing independence; adolescence (teenage years) by an innate desire to separate and couple and push boundaries. The journey is often depicted as a ladder with rungs; we climb upwards.

Having an idea of these different stages will give you a deeper understanding of your own personal report. This axis of mental development – the period from birth to adulthood – is our model for measuring the subconscious because, of all the best psychological, psychotherapeutic and psychiatric theories and models that already exist, they have stood the test of time. This is the most robustly evidenced model onto which we could map the unconscious slip and, from there, measure an individual's capacity to recover. This developmental trajectory through childhood has been recognised and built on from the ancient Greeks right through to modern neuroscientists. As we grow, we pass mental developmental milestones that parallel our physical developmental milestones, and each is a separate state of mind. So let's have a look at them.

Babyhood

Babies, in essence, are dependent; they cannot be independent. The classic (if slightly simplistic) understanding is that babies are dependent, and weaning children are learning that they exist as separate people who have boundaries between themselves and others. There comes a point where our physical development is sufficient for us to begin to have an awareness that we are not a part of another's being. We notice the absence or presence of our carer, whether they put on a hat or glasses, which changes their appearance, or we sense a difference of body smell. However, before a baby reaches this stage, the absence of our carer is not cognitively recognised but is emotionally felt as deprivation. For example, with the absence of milk, a baby does not know that it is hungry. All it knows is that it is in pain, and that pain can feel like an attack.

If you are abandoned when you are too small to feed yourself, you die. That terrible fear of being abandoned, of falling when no one is there to catch you, is crucial to the developmental building blocks of the mind. When you are born and you connect with soft, warm food and the heartbeat of a person you are familiar with, then expectations have been met. If you don't find that, then expectations have not been met, and you have already formed your perception of the world. That early sense of need and abandonment creates all sorts of emotional feelings which feed into a state of mind. It is not just the dependency, it is the fear of losing that on which your life depends, and the consequences of that.

We believe that these very early developmental stages are linked to inexpressible anger when young, which can lead to shame later, because if the separation doesn't occur we learn that we don't have a right to exist as a separate person. The anger arises because we innately know that we do have a right to exist, but we don't have the capacity at this age to put into words why we are angry. We know that we should trust our carers to help us make the next step, but if they do not do so, we become ashamed for existing. In our minds we are unworthy children, because we cannot yet believe that our parents are fallible.

It is during this period that a baby's implicit memories are laid down. Implicit memory is remembered at the time of growing, but once some time has elapsed, the memory is not easily accessible. At the age of four or five, we do not explicitly remember events from before the age of three, unless they were particularly traumatic. That is why, when working with people who are struggling with their wellbeing and mental health, it's not only about their memories. Often, what troubles us all is not what we can remember. It is about wanting to be understood and then finding insight into the way our individual mind perceives the world. This can start the journey to health.

The Toddler Years

The toddler stage is marked by a sense of omnipotence and the instinct to wipe out any competition. So a little child will say, 'Yes, I love my baby brother and now could you vacuum him up?' Lots of things are happening inside the toddler's brain but they don't have the words to talk about them. As a parent, you can answer, 'Yes, I know the baby is taking up my time, but I love you very much and it will be alright.' The child is then able to process their difficult feelings into normal, ordinary feelings which can be dealt with and negotiated, and neither parent, child nor sibling is wiped out with rage. If the parent screams when the toddler bites the baby, the toddler, who must of course be restrained, does not have its legitimate feelings – of anger at having to share parental time – recognised. This leads to a growing inability to grieve at losing part of the parent to another. Such unresolved grief becomes stuck in the mind and the toddler cannot recover. However, fortunately, most children manage to process the grief and thus recover, emerging on the other side with joy and love.

The other cardinal feature of toddlerhood is the capacity to fantasise that we are big, then coming back to Earth and realising that we are small. We are finding our way to cut loose from the apron strings without being run over. Being small can be humiliating, but we can learn to tolerate that feeling and not pass it on to others if we ourselves are not mocked in our learning endeavours.

The Oedipal Phase

Next, a child will develop through what is technically called the Oedipal phase of childhood. This is where we learn to couple with another person; however, we cannot actually achieve this at this age because the physical mechanisms and hormonal triggers for desire that are necessary for coupling are not yet fully in place. Little children will jump into bed between parents and push one or other parent away so that they can pretend to be the other grown-up in the pair. They are practising coupling and are actually gaining a good emotional understanding of what is necessary for a healthy relationship once their physical capability develops.

In physical terms, most of our milk teeth have long since emerged by now. There is much truth in Aristotle's words, 'Give me the child until he is seven and I will show you the man' – once a child reaches this age, they are capable of surviving alone if they have to. The basis of the mind is largely formed, so the way we see life and develop relationships is already laid down – what comes after is built upon those foundations.

Latency

After the age of seven, a child wants facts, rules, information; there is little symbolic thinking yet. So, if the rule says 'don't play football in the sitting room', this is taken literally – the rule doesn't say anything about tennis! At this point, a child can develop a healthy relationship with authority, where they know they are their own person but can also learn from others with more experience. Sometimes, however, their mind develops in such a way that they have to please authority all the time. This may be because there is a lack of trust of authority, and they feel they must please because the authority has responded in a way that they feel might 'destroy' them. Psychologically, this may be how the response feels. They therefore make sure that this does not happen, ensuring also that their own destructive capacity is tucked away so as not to destroy the person on whom they are dependent.

Sometimes, the child may feel that the adult is not acting in their best interests, though claiming they are, in which case a mistrust of authority enters the dynamic and the child may rebel too early, always defaulting to the opposite path from that requested by the adult. This leaves the child without a secure internal awareness of their own needs.

Adolescence

The next step is adolescence, which in psychological terms has a meaning quite different from the current idea of western teenage behaviour. This step is about the desire to go out and build a relationship, with the essential and eventual aim of coupling. Out of this relationship will come something which is unimaginably different from the couple, but a product of both of them. Adolescence is the drive to create something new by becoming a part of a couple, rather than to self-replicate. It is about the establishment of a new tribe.

This true meaning of the term adolescence is apparent worldwide in some cultures, where life expectancy is shorter. The teenagers of the tribe will couple, procreate and take over the parental roles of hunter, farmer and provider much earlier in their lives than in other cultures. In western society, the idea of marrying and starting one's own tribe at seventeen is less common, but this reflects a westernised restriction on the adolescent drive, which delays their transition to adulthood. This can give rise to the frustration that is the source of much of the conflict between western adolescents and adults. What we sometimes have today, with the caricature of stroppy teenagers who don't want parents in their face, is a second toddlerhood, not an adolescence.

Adulthood

An adult state of mind comes when we start to harness our adolescent creative state of mind, rather than squashing or condemning it. Adult characteristics include the capacity to fully empathise, to have responsibility for ourselves and others, to see and accept the consequences of our own actions and to allow others who are near us to be powerful. A mature adult is also able to accept the limits of their own mortality, which leads to risk aversion – which is why really good leaders need, in their adult make-up, a good dose of the adolescent capacity to take considered risks in order to move forward.

The Importance of Your 'Internal Parent' and 'Unconscious Family'

There is a reason why we talk so much about different developmental stages and your unconscious age. All your different characteristics do not exist in a vacuum – they exist in a matrix of unconscious checks and balances and are only activated when provoked in certain circumstances. The key thing is, do you have an internal parent? Have you been able to take positive comments and experiences with others and learn from them in order to construct an internal parent or friend, or have you only taken on board the harsher things and so have ended up with an internal critic or judge? The more we have good internal parents, friends, siblings, the more resilient we are, because when we are alone, the 'good parent' is inside us and is there to help us. But if harsher or more fragile responses have been formed and taken on board, and we are feeling alone, the things inside will not be helpful, and will not be a comfort.

When people talk about low self-esteem, what they often mean is that they do not have this internal friend or parent to soothe them and help them to get through things. Instead, some people have very harsh and bitter internal critics who whip and beat them on (workaholics can be like this). This is not healthy because those around them, usually a child or a partner, end up holding on to all the emotion and loss; it gets shunted onto them. They then have to hold it for the adult or they get pushed out of the way as the person pushes forward, leaving damage in their wake. This lack of self-esteem exists where there is a lack of the inner resource to help someone get through the difficult times.

In the throes of a tantrum, little children will often throw their teddies or soft toys downstairs as opposed to taking them to bed with them and allowing them to be a part of their companionship. A frustrated parent might say, 'I'm not going to pick up your toy; it's the third time you have thrown it downstairs.' This may seem reasonable, but actually what the child needs to know is that the parent understands that the child is angry with them but they can't find a way to express why. Once the parent helps the child express what it is they are angry about, the child is likely to stop throwing the teddy downstairs. Eventually the toy becomes virtual as it is internalised; this is reflected in its progress from the bed to the chair, so that by the time we are adults, we have developed our own companionship within. If a partner still has a toy on the bed, it is a sure sign that they still struggle with their kind internal friend, and that they still have to find that outside themselves. They are probably quite resilient while someone is playing that role, but should that person leave, their resilience might start to break down.

Your Internal and External Scaffolding

Internal scaffolding is built in the mind as a tiny baby being cradled in their parents' arms, or swaddled in blankets to give a physical sense of security by external containment. As the child grows through the steps of weaning, separation and independence, they internalise that swaddling and develop a scaffolding that mimics the security that they have been offered in the external world.

Each of us has our own unique internal scaffolding, derived from our predisposition and our upbringing. Since birth, your mind has been building this subconscious internal scaffolding, piece by piece, so that by the time you are an adult you have your own internal structure of mind, which is like an 'internal home'. A combination of good boundaries, discipline and love will tend to promote a robust construction of this internal scaffolding, but if bits of this internal structure have not been put in an 'appropriate' place, or not built securely, it is very hard to dismantle this scaffolding when you reach adulthood.

Along the way, we may also find that we have to prop up what is missing or 'inappropriate' with external scaffolding. The mind is flexible and will have adapted itself around the missing or poorly built parts so that it can continue to work. These 'work-arounds' are your coping or survival mechanisms. So, for example, you can be obsessively tidy in order to hide and manage your internal chaos, or alternatively you can be totally chaotic in order to communicate to the world that you are chaotic inside. The problem with external scaffolding is that it is much easier to challenge and damage than internal scaffolding. Having a secure internal scaffold is the best form of wellbeing. It enables us to propel ourselves back up the ladder when we have slipped down through the childhood state of mind.

As adults, we are able to spend most of our waking hours in a 'mature' state at the top of the ladder because our internal scaffolding is secure. But from time to time we all slip back down the ladder to an earlier developmental stage. Our unconscious family, which lives inside all of us and derives from our experiences in life, comes into play much more irrationally the further down the ladder we slip and the longer we stay in a space in which we can't recover our more adult state of mind.

As we have already mentioned, this kind of experience is common to all of us and is a part of our everyday lives. There are a thousand different stimuli for a human being that can, in a second, knock us from the calm suited-and-booted adult person coming into the workplace and back down temporarily to a lower stage on the ladder. Everybody descends the ladder dozens of times a day – it is impossible not to. As we've said, what matters is whether we get stuck in the state of childhood (neediness), or adolescence (grumpiness), for example, for a significant period of time, or whether we make a swift recovery.

Freud had a theory that the primitive part of us (the so-called reptile brain, housed in the amygdala) comes up to 'bite' us when we are under pressure, taking over the more sophisticated part of our brain so that we no longer have any control. With The Cambridge Code, we wanted to develop this idea and go beyond it. We focused on the constantly changing pattern of slips and recoveries up and down the developmental ladder. Each person has their own pattern that is unique to them, which can be caught in a measurement: the place to which we default on the ladder in response to a certain stimulus, and the speed with which we bounce back to the adult resting state. Characterising and quantifying the way that we slip and bounce-back – our patterns – provides us with the potential to see in an immediate snapshot what might previously have taken hours of therapeutic analysis. This is where The Cambridge Code comes in.

The Cambridge Code captures the moment when the subconscious mind is provoked into a space that is not its usual adult space; it measures that slip and then takes account of the speed of recovery.

Developing The Cambridge Code:
The Methodology Behind the Idea

Once we recognised that this movement up and down the development axis contained great potential to observe and quantify unconscious behavioural characteristics, The Cambridge Code team set their minds to designing a method of interpreting these patterns. Work began with a team of scientists from Cambridge University in 2013. As well as looking at all the best psychological, psychotherapeutic and psychiatric theories, we studied a large body of research from the last 150 years – from Freud, Piaget and Erikson, to Ainsworth, and most recently to Hepworth-Target, Fonagy and Siegel: those who have mapped the existence of stages of human development and models of the mind. The considerable breadth and depth of our research made it possible for us to translate and condense psychotherapeutic experiences into a series of questions and scenarios that would make up The Cambridge Code tool.

Phase One: Drawing Up the Questions

In the first phase, we identified appropriate triggers that would prompt slips from an individual's normal resting state of mind. These 'slips', as we have seen, can be provoked by asking someone to recall a certain incident and then assessing their response through a combination of factual recall and self-analysis. After testing some 5,000 questions, and following these up with more than

1,000 full clinical sessions, a prototype questionnaire tool was drawn up.

The questionnaire was designed with a variety of different types of question that are intended to nudge your subconscious. Consider this settling-in question from The Code: 'When you were a child, did you fight with your siblings?' The question will take different people back to different stages on the developmental ladder. For some, they will remember a particular period of their childhood when fighting was common and they will slip to that level of childhood for a few moments while they reminisce. Others may have a sister who went through an illness just a few years ago, and they will return to that particular time, perhaps becoming emotional as they remember the support they needed to give. Others may not have any siblings, but will instead be reminded of extended family or close friends with whom they fought. They might remember a particular fight at school and wonder what that friend is doing right now.

Crucially, there is no right or wrong answer. It is important to remember this throughout the questionnaire. This first question is designed to nudge or prompt you to explore your subconscious. It is not scored and the data from the answer is not important; it is your response to and the way you feel about it that sets the tone for the next part of the questionnaire. Different people slip to different levels and stay there for varying lengths of time. Subsequent questions will hone in on specific scenarios that have been devised with great care to allow analysis and scoring both for the degree of slip and the speed of recovery. It's likely that you won't recall each of these scenarios, as the prompts are for your subconscious, rather than your conscious, mind. You might also find that, for these particular question examples, after completing the questionnaire, you have a strong urge to connect with the person about whom the prompts caused you to think.

The questionnaire has been carefully designed to cover sections of the developmental ladder, and to allow for combinations of responses that correlate with the understanding we have on different mental developmental stages. The prototype questionnaire was trialled on an initial cohort of 540 participants, with follow-up clinical interviews. We were excited when we saw that the raw data appeared to confirm that The Cambridge Code team had worked out how to measure the unique patterns of unconscious slip and recovery.

Phase Two: Interpreting the Answers

For the second phase of development, we needed to design a system for reliably translating numerical scores from the questionnaire into a picture of the individual's characteristics. For this, a two-stage algorithm was designed: the first stage was developed to assign the individual a score that reflected their states of mind and rates of recovery, as noted above; then the second stage was developed, using clinical case studies and trials, to correlate the composite scores with a selection of subconscious characteristics, identified through our extensive market research.

The tool was trialled on carefully identified individuals known to exhibit particularly strong characteristics in specific areas – for example, resilience, rivalry, empathy, etc. Subsequently, professors from Harvard University and the Massachusetts Institute of Technology (MIT) provided independent live-trial validation to corroborate our findings.

Phase Three: Identifying the Domains

Designing the coding paradigms, or patterns, was a complex process. Initially, we identified around 150 of these different aspects of the mind because of the complexity of the mind and its subconscious characteristics. We call these aspects 'domains'. Subsequently, we streamlined these into approximately forty main areas and from there we refined them further into the twelve domains that are most applicable, relevant and fundamental to personal and professional wellbeing.

These twelve fundamental domains do not exist as entities in isolation, but co-exist in an interactive framework. Some domain types occur frequently in combination, others appear together only rarely. The expression of some domain types can be limited in their potential growth over the years by the existence of others; some brains are not restricted in this manner. For each reader, the individual profile of your unique subconscious is the product of your coding for all twelve domains.

The simple descriptions provided in this book – for example, competitiveness or resilience (see Part Two: Exploring the Domains) – establish a framework by which we can characterise and differentiate between the domains, to simplify the analysis of the subconscious tendencies that are revealed.

Phase Four: Evolving Versions from Corporate to Wellbeing

The initial version of the questionnaire tool was designed specifically for use in career, team and personal development. Subsequently, we developed another version of the tool, for use as a wellbeing screen, and we continue to adapt The Code for numerous other uses, including market predictive analytics, dating and relationship products, as well as diversity and inclusion in recruitment.

However, while trialling and refining these different versions, we were increasingly struck by the universal interest shown by the trial subjects in receiving and discussing their results. The concept of understanding one's unique subconscious mind seemed to resonate with the audience to an unexpected degree. And so the idea took shape that The Code should be adapted into a format that was accessible to the general public, focusing on its relevance to day-to-day wellbeing. The questionnaire you have now has been specifically designed and enhanced to focus on your wellbeing – specifically in the key areas of relationships, the family and the workplace.

With the process refined and complete, The Cambridge Code was launched. In an age when it is possible for an individual to request a DNA genetic profile by mail order, we have now made it possible for someone to request a profile of their subconscious mind, and complete the assessment online, in under thirty minutes. Many thousands of people have now completed The Cambridge Code tool and improved their understanding of themselves and, by extension, their overall wellbeing.

Key Code Concepts

Here are some key things to keep in mind when looking at your report and reading through the book.

The Green and The Blue – Why There is No Such Thing as a 'Good' or 'Bad' Domain

When you get your report, you will see that The Code will give you either a 'green' or a 'blue' result for each domain.

The 'green' domain represents the moderate presentation of the domain. The 'blue' domain represents a deeper or more concentrated presentation of the domain, but they are not binary. The blue domain is actually composed of two 'flipsides', which both have the same blue root but which can look like opposites. Imagine a horseshoe, with the two ends curving away from the bottom of the cup shape and then coming back together until they almost touch. Imagine also that the horseshoe is coloured deep green in the bottom of the cup, and shading into deep blue on both sides as the colour moves towards each end. They have the same root, but they take different directions. These are the two different aspects of blue. An example might be where one partner is very tidy and the other is not. The one who is tidy might be so because they are trying to 'tidy' their untidy mind. The one who is untidy might also have an untidy mind, but tries to express it by being untidy in their environment. This is why, at the beginning of each chapter, there are summaries for two blue seeming opposites and one green.

It is not the case that a green domain equates with 'good' and a blue domain with 'bad' or vice versa. The codes are not pejorative.

Variety here is absolutely the spice of life. Many of life's most inter-esting, engaging and productive individuals exhibit a smattering of blue domain types. Sometimes a profusion. Conversely, it is often the case that a team that struggles to leap forward creatively is found to be overwhelmingly green domain in their overall make-up.

You Can't Cheat The Code!

We anticipate that you will find the online questionnaire easy to complete. Quite a few people have told us they tried to cheat The Code – it's human nature! The way in which the questionnaire is designed and cross-coordinated with multiple algorithms means that it would be pretty much impossible to aim for a certain result.

This is because there is no single question that links to a par-ticular brain type – all coding questions offer input on multiple outputs. Some are 'settling-in questions', as mentioned before, writ-ten to put you into a particular frame of mind or on a particular rung of the developmental ladder. For instance, we do not neces-sarily numerically code for where you are in the birth order within your family; rather, in asking this, we aim to ease you into thinking about your childhood in general.

You may find that, annoyingly, there is often no answer that you want to give – the team know that, but they are nudging your sub-conscious to give an answer and are interested in how you react to that process. It's similar to the way we 'slip' and 'recover'. The team had an experience with a professor when attending a meeting to discuss the development of our groundbreaking work in imaging the DNA of the unconscious mind. He came down the stairs after doing The Cambridge Code and was literally shaking his laptop with frustration. 'There is no answer I want to give!' The irrational four-year-old had been provoked into being, as, although there were plenty of valid answers, none of them showed him in a perfect light. He laughed and was generously self-aware enough to acknowledge the developmental slip into a perfectionist state of mind.

Understanding Your Results

The results of your assessment include an analytical synopsis (rather like a medical specialist interpreting your blood tests) that aims to provide you with an understanding of yourself at your core. In conjunction with this book, your report gives suggestions for areas of self-exploration and some takeaway tips for key life areas: relationships, family and the workplace. It gives you a chance to consider why you make the choices you do – why you might always choose a certain kind of partner, or a certain kind of job, or why others react to you in a particular way. Some sections of the report may be less relevant than other sections in your current phase of life, but circumstances may change, as you leave home, get new jobs, develop relationships, have children and grow old.

This self-knowledge might at first be a little uncomfortable – it can be difficult to have previously unknown deep-seated and subconscious drivers revealed in a matter of minutes – but with the self-knowledge that The Code provides, you might be able to better understand the origin of this discomfort.

Using This Book to Decode Your Results

The online test is designed for brevity and accuracy. As with a DNA readout, the book puts your results in context, to provide depth and understanding to the information. It acts, in effect, as the 'consultation' that supports your DNA testing.

Each domain has its own chapter, which explains its relevance to your everyday life and discusses the ways in which this domain may manifest, illustrated with real-life case histories and anecdotes. You may find these amusing, sad, poignant or resonant. All, incidentally, are true, although the contributors' names have been changed. It may be of interest to some readers to have an explanation of the formative processes that influence the development of each particular brain domain, so we have therefore chosen to include a section in each chapter on the psychological origin of the brain type.

The book is designed to complement and enhance your online report, adding an extra dimension to your understanding of your subconscious traits. The chapters can also offer insight into the subconscious minds of those close to you: partners, family, friends, colleagues. For this reason, the suggested self-exploration and takeaway tips in the book are broader than the personal feedback of the online report: you are encouraged to consider not only your own brain type but the manner in which it interacts with the other brain types in your orbit.

A final word before you dive in: unlocking your subconscious can be a profound experience and you might want to consider sharing your new understanding with those around you. The insights can trigger a shift in your relationships which may be ultimately rewarding, but the process of change itself can also be unsettling. You might encourage those close to you to read this book, or just share with them edited, relevant highlights. You may even decide to unlock your subconscious together as a team. No one way is better than another.

As we said at the beginning, 'so much easier to look under another's swirling sea than the one we are in ourselves.' Now, with the development of The Cambridge Code, there is a tool to help you to visualise your own swirling depths.

Frequently Asked Questions

Is one domain better than the other? Is the blue domain bad?
As we've said, The Code is not pejorative. The 'green' domain represents the moderate presentation of the domain. The 'blue' domain represents a deeper, or more concentrated presentation of the domain. It's true that having a blue domain may mean there are certain areas that you may wish to try to be conscious of when stressful life events occur, but these characteristics can also be extremely useful qualities in certain circumstances and are an important part of who you are.

Can't I just pick answers that make me look 'good'?
The Code is deliberately designed to be easy to complete. There's often no answer that seems like the 'socially desirable' option, and no single question links to a particular domain type, so trying to cherry-pick answers that you think will give you a certain colour brain is near impossible.

Which of the questions relate to the different domains?
No single question links to a particular domain type and not all the questions are actually coded – some are there for 'settling-in' and are written to put you into a particular frame of mind.

Some of the questions are quite personal – who will see my results?
The actual answers you give to each of the questions will never be seen by anybody else – not even the team at The Cambridge Code.

They are used to drive a complex set of algorithms which turn them into a map of your subconscious mind – and, as no one single question links to an individual characteristic, it's impossible to figure out what you answered for a particular question by looking at your profile.

How do I get my results?
Once you've completed The Code, you'll automatically see an onscreen profile of your subconscious mind. Your results are presented to you as a dashboard of the twelve fundamental brain areas, with a short explanation of what the colour coding means for you, accessible by clicking on each domain.

I've got my results; what should I do next?
The Code isn't there to tell you what to do, but to throw light on the core of yourself – your instinctive responses and thoughts. It is designed to help you understand why you make the choices you do, and consider if there are other choices that might suit you better, or that you might wish to make instead. Simply knowing this can be enough for some people to make changes, but others may wish to call on friends or family for help.

What do I do – there's no answer that I want to give to the questions?
The questions have been carefully written to get you to think about a range of different situations – and to examine how these would make you feel, and how you might act as a result. You may find that there is often no answer that you want to give – and the team know that! But the questions will press your subconscious to give an answer and your response is critical to how the algorithm interprets your reaction to that process.

Should I share my results with other people?
It's totally up to you. Some people will want to keep them private, others may instinctively wish to share them with others to ask if they seem accurate, or perhaps to enlist their help to make changes in a particular area. Giving others an insight into your subconscious may also help them to engage with you in a way that best suits your needs.

Is it true that opposites attract, and if so, how does this work with the domains?
The key for all couple attraction is that two blues are most likely to attract. They are opposites in external ways but underneath they have a similar foundation to their external way of responding to others. So someone very needy may well be attracted to someone who never seems to need anyone and is always there for them, but the being there for someone does in its own way serve that person's underlying needs without them having to show them to the world. Green is more likely to be attracted to green.

Part Two | **Exploring the Domains**

The following sections will guide you through each of the domains to help you understand your own personal profile in detail. There are, as we have mentioned, twelve domains and these are listed with page numbers for easy reference. You can read them in order, or choose the ones of most interest to you:

Each chapter represents a different area of the mind and the way it grows, and these are represented here as domains. They are based in an understanding of the developmental ladder and the way in which the internal scaffolding of our mind is created through pre-disposition and our lived experiences. That is why so much of each of the following chapters contains analogy and illustration from the childhood language. If some of it leaves you feeling that you haven't had experience of children, remember that you yourself were once a child. The Cambridge Code aims to help us get in touch with the myriad complex feelings we carry with us throughout our lives, some of which we know about and some of which we hide even from ourselves. Babyhood and smallness is where we all begin, even if we don't always want to think about it when we are bigger and stronger. It can be very appealing to be looked after again, to have no responsibilities, but it can also be very disturbing to feel dependent and powerless. The sense of who we were and how we experienced life never leaves us.

Competitiveness

Do you believe that, if you had been able to do something,
it would hypothetically have been better than anybody else's
effort? Do you shut down and do more listening than talking
about yourself when someone is being competitive with you?
Do you step out of the competition in a fit of generosity, to
let someone else win, but then resent it later?

Or are you proud of yourself and able to say when you have
done something good, and then it's about a personal best
rather than a comparison with someone else?

Consider the scenario: two children are running a long-distance race at a school sports day. They find themselves neck-and-neck at the front of the field, both pushing themselves as hard as possible. One stumbles and falls. The other carries on and wins the race. He is showing typical rivalrous spirit and determination to win.

Now consider an alternative outcome: when one child falls, the other stops, extends their hand and pulls their competitor back to their feet. A less rivalrous spirit, showing more empathy towards their peers. Or, a third possible outcome: same children, same race, but one deliberately sticks out a leg to trip up the other. They carry on to win the race. This is an example of an over-competitive nature, where there is a need to win at any cost, and where even a cheated win is regarded as a positive outcome.

Rivalrous situations such as these are played out throughout our lives and in all aspects of our personal and work relationships. Welcome to the competitive domain!

Where does competitiveness come from?

We are all born with a competitive streak. It is a survival mechanism. In a world of dangers, hungry siblings and maternal distraction, the baby that screams the loudest gets heard. How you manage your own competitive streak depends on the circumstances you find yourself in. It will probably come as no surprise that sibling rivalry or the experience of being an only child plays an important formative role in our competitive coding. That's why questions about birth order and sibling age gap tend to feature early in most psychotherapeutic interactions (and are early 'settling-in' questions within our Cambridge Code diagnostic tool). If you are an only child, you may spot the frustration of answering 'not applicable' to some of the questions about siblings. This is a frustration that siblings are used to. Though siblings may provoke jealousy, sometimes those frustrations are harder if you haven't had the experience of having to wait for a younger brother or sister to be ready to leave before going to the playground, for example.

The influence of parenting is an important factor as well. Parents sometimes feel that they must always be fair to each child, treating everyone the same. In practice this is impossible, because everyone is not the same and they are not the same parents when the next child is born. Trying to achieve this equality can create an incredible amount of stress within families, as can the other extreme, where one child is favoured. Parents unwittingly can have a particular affiliation with a particular child at a particular moment in time. It is not necessarily the same child forever, but often a moving rollercoaster, depending on the child's age or the vulnerability with which the parent has identified at that moment. In a sense this is good parenting: parents can empathetically move from vulnerable child to vulnerable child as and when they are needed by them, in different ways. After all, babies are more vulnerable than twelve-year-olds. And we can see our own vulnerability in a child at any given time, but we can also become hooked into imagining what that child must feel by superimposing what we felt many years ago into the present scenario. This can affect how we behave.

So, a parent walks through the door after a day at work and two children who have been happily playing together suddenly start to fight. They are effectively fighting over the parent (though it may not look like that) for time and attention. Where, minutes before, they were aligned buddies, the second the key is in the door they become rivals. It is quite common for parents to identify more with one child than another in this situation, depending on how their parents behaved towards them when they were young.

It is interesting to understand one's own past rivalry with siblings because it helps to understand the reasons why you might back one child against another in a fight. It is not uncommon to look at a pair of children and think, 'X picked the fight, but it seems that Y is always the one who gets into trouble.' This may be because of past form – maybe X usually picks the fight and so they have that reputation – but more often than not it is because the parent imagines themselves as either the vulnerable one or as the strong one, and identifies back through time. A parent over-engaging with one particular child throughout their childhood can lead to situations of spectacular lifelong rivalry between siblings.

The more the little one is protected, the more violent the rage inside the older one, and the more aggressive they get. A balance is needed to allow the older one to work out their grief so that they both come out healthy at the other end with the pecking order established, and the older one doesn't become emotionally stuck. There are adults who are ragingly jealous of their younger siblings for things that no one else around them can see, but they know. No parent will ever really win that one, because it is impossible to deny the reality of a child being pushed out of baby's place, but it is probably better to try to understand it than stop it completely.

A child who shows their rivalry by biting is often acting out something they don't have. Interestingly, they will rarely bite the obviously enviable child. So they won't bite the child who has twenty-six cars (because everyone envies them), but they bite the child who has the pink car, which they don't have. The self-identification is close enough to feel at one with them and to feel an unconscious rage that, all things being equal, they should be the same.

The teenage years are to a great extent defined by competition. The whole of adolescence is essentially a rivalrous developmental melting pot in which the teenager competes for a place in the adult world. Sexual, academic and sporting rivalries abound, and shape our competitive brain marker. As we mature into adults, we carry this competitive marker into all aspects of our relationships, families and workplaces.

POINTS TO CONSIDER:

- It is normal for siblings to be rivalrous with each other, competing for the time and attention of their parents. You may recall this as a prominent feature of your own childhood. You may be aware of sibling rivalry persisting into adulthood.

- If you are the parent of multiple children, avoid over-engaging with one particular child. Try to understand why you particularly identify with that child.
- When looking back to your own teenage years, can you appreciate that rivalrous behaviour towards parents is a crucial feature of teenage development and growth? If you have regular interaction with teenage children, you may need to continue reminding yourself of this.

Competitiveness in everyday life

A healthy competitive spirit is a force for good. It can be harnessed within work teams and families to enable growth and improvement. If you have blue coding in this domain you may tip into over-rivalrous behaviour, where there is a desire to stunt the growth of a rival or even to inflict damage in order to win. It's the equivalent of sticking your foot out in the cross-country race. In its extreme form, this can manifest as the need to physically harm the other. Or, less extremely, to opt to delete them on your social media.

In the workplace, we might instinctively expect companies to do well if they are filled with competitive employees. However, this approach is self-limiting. The over-rivalrous employee may be too threatened to hire in good workers and could end up with a substandard team. An over-rivalrous team may behave destructively towards each other, limiting the growth of other team members. Interestingly, entrepreneurs often have insight into their rivalrous nature and accommodate it by working in a solo environment where the issue of having a rival doesn't come up.

Rivalrous behaviour in the workplace may be readily recognisable, but there are other occasions on which it may manifest more subtly. Children, for example, often manage rivalry by walking away: they will bait the group and then exit, saying, 'I'm not playing this game anymore.' This kind of behaviour can translate into the work environment as, 'I'm not working with you anymore' – for example, leaving a staff meeting at a crucial moment.

In the sporting arena, too, those with a strong presentation of rivalry may need to apply some restraint. The competitive domain is usually strongly expressed in high-level sportsmen, but training and experience enable them to channel their competitive spirit in an appropriate manner: rivalry between teams is a more useful driver than rivalry within the team. We see from time to time how a prod from the opposition leads to an angry outburst on the pitch. The red card will serve to provide some additional external control.

One partner may always need to have the last word; the other allows it (see The Rivalrous Couple case study, page 43). But even with this matched pairing, rivalry between a partner and a friendship group may be a common cause of friction.

So you might have a situation where one partner goes out for dinner in the evening with a group of friends. The other, who chose to remain at home, nevertheless phones repeatedly with 'vitally important' messages. 'Did you mean to leave your keys at home? Do you have any idea where the baby's teddy is? Just letting you know that your mother has phoned . . .' Suddenly there are six vitally important things that have to happen and, instead of drawing a boundary, the other partner keeps picking up the calls and they both end up in a temper. This is a form of 'killing off' the rival, where the excluded one has to intrude, even if they didn't want to go to the dinner. In a relationship, there is usually one who is sensitive to exclusion and one who is sensitive to being intruded upon. The one who is sensitive to being intruded upon will always tend to slightly exclude because that keeps them safe. But this sets up an even greater desire in the one sensitive to exclusion to intrude!

At the beginning of a new romantic relationship, constant phone calls and texts are part and parcel of the normal 'madness' of love. But if this pattern of behaviour continues, it may reflect excessive rivalry rather than love. You know you love to win, but it takes true generosity to allow your partner or friends to win at times when they need it. If it continues, ask yourself if that is love, or rivalry. Try to consciously observe yourself symbolically 'killing off rivals' to see that you are doing this, rather than justifying it with hundreds of different reasons.

Case Study: The Rivalrous Couple

One couple profiled for The Cambridge Code described how, in their early days of seeing each other, they had taken a drive to the coast. As they rounded the crest of a hill, the beautiful coast-line came into view. 'Wow, that's gorgeous,' said Ben, chilled as always. 'Yes, but I saw it first,' said Joanna (incidentally, a high-level athlete).

People who don't allow their spouse to go out with their friends may unconsciously want to get rid of the rivals. But rather than saying, 'Go and have a good time with your friends, I'm kind of tired tonight', or 'I'll come too, I'd like them to be my friends', they manoeuvre the situation to prevent the other having any other life except with them. It is based on their fear of not being able to win against any other rival, but it damages the relationship anyway and the battle is not won.

People often have a high level of insight about their own competitiveness. It is not so much a question of what colour your coding is, but the control you choose to exert over it. In some cases, you may make a conscious choice to suppress your competitive characteristic, for fear that others will dislike it. As a result, you may tend to distance yourselves from events, becoming an observer rather than a participant. In other cases, you may be able to acknowledge that you are locking horns with a rival and deliberately choose to modify your behaviour. You extend the hand in the race, rather than sticking out the foot.

Case Study: The Freud Brothers

Clement and Lucian Freud, the grandsons of the famous psychoanalyst Sigmund Freud, were said to have fallen out over who was the winner of a boyhood race. One version of the story has it that the pair were running through the park, with Clement in the lead. Lucian shouted out 'Stop thief', at which point a passer-by apprehended Clement and Lucian sprinted ahead to victory. The spat developed into a lifelong rift. Not such a successful case of rivalry.

If you code green for competitiveness

A green for this domain indicates a balanced competitive nature. You are able to compete in order to achieve, but you work well in a team or relationship without being over-rivalrous with your peers. You are not threatened by the success of others, and you have the capacity to encourage others to flourish.

Competitiveness in Relationships – Green

You are balanced for this domain marker, but it is important to realise that your partner or friends may not be. Give consideration to issues that may be thrown up by a more rivalrous partner or friend.

EXPLORE:

- Can you balance your own wishes and those of others?
- Can you allow a certain amount of healthy conflict with those closest to you?
- Do you feel that your steadiness curbs your creativity?

TIPS:

- Others might be envious of your balanced capacity and you may need to manage feelings about this within yourself.
- Healthy conflict is one of your strengths – use it wherever you can.
- Be on the lookout for those situations in which you can express your creativity by taking a risk.

Competitiveness in the Family – Green

Although you yourself are not overly competitive, there will be rivalrous patterns that emerge as part of the normal family dynamic. When dealing with competitive children or siblings, it may help to try to understand any underlying issues of envy.

EXPLORE:

- What were your own childhood experiences of sibling rivalry?
- Do you sufficiently defend your own position in the family? Even with siblings, stepchildren, in-laws, etc?
- In family life, do you feel that the other members of the family are the 'fun' ones?

TIPS:

- You may well want to be the referee – a good place to be – but on occasion try another role.
- Holding out the hand at the end of a match helps manage feelings of winning or losing. Can you find the equivalent gesture in your family arguments?
- Watch out that you don't submerge your own fun and humour in maintaining a balance for everybody else.

Competitiveness in the Workplace – Green

Your balanced competitive nature in many ways makes you an ideal employee. You will be good at hiring in at the right level and will drive projects forward in the appropriate manner. Your challenges may arise in knowing how to interact with overly competitive colleagues.

EXPLORE:

- Are you always as proactive as you could be in work situations?
- How robustly are you able to stand up for your views in front of colleagues?
- How do you respond to very competitive colleagues?

TIPS:

- Engage and compete more fully in work situations – it may increase your productivity.
- You may need to promote productive rivalry within the team more than you would naturally tolerate.
- If necessary, seek advice/training on how to optimise team dynamics.

If you code blue for competitiveness

You have a highly competitive element to your personality. You have the drive to succeed, but at times this may be at the expense of others. You may flourish in individual pursuits or sporting activities, but you may need to work harder to be a better team player and team leader. Your competitive tendencies may occasionally manifest in frictional relationships with family members and loved ones.

Competitiveness in Relationships – Blue

Do you always need to be right? Do you always have to have the last word? Do you compete for your partner's attention? Sometimes you may even compete for a child's love and affection. These scenarios can act out in two ways: trying to get the attention, and preventing another from getting it. It is more about getting rid of rivals than stepping up and claiming the affection.

Case Study: The Competitive Grandfather

A daughter came to visit her mother, bringing her first baby. The baby was fractious, so the grandmother suggested taking the baby for a walk in the park. The daughter was keen and went off to get the baby ready in its buggy. The grandmother asked the grandfather to come along. He appeared enthusiastic and put down his newspaper. At the door, however, he seemed to stumble on the doorstep and insisted on being helped back to his chair. He required tea and sympathy from his wife, while his daughter went out alone with the baby.

EXPLORE:

- Do you always need to be right? Do you always have to have the last word?
- If your partner went out for the evening with a group of friends, would you feel excluded? Would you make an excuse to interrupt their evening?

Or,

- Do you step out of conflict situations because you are afraid of them?

TIPS:

- Don't be afraid to seek out people who challenge you. It may be very difficult but it might in the end be stimulating.
- Remember that your partner's friendship groups are important. See if you can find ways to manage your understandable jealousy.

- If you step out of conflict, try to be less afraid of your own secret competitiveness and step up.

Competitiveness in the Family – Blue

Parents who come up blue in this characteristic may not often experience conflict with their children while the child is small and poses no competitive threat. However, when the child reaches teenage years and begins to fight for its place in the adult world, conflict can arise very quickly, as the teenage child is now seen as a rival.

When families are still young and growing, children might be over-rivalrous with each other, fighting for time and attention. Typically, a child will interpose its head between their parents or between parents and others, to block the rival, in one of many forms of 'blocking' behaviour.

When faced with rivalrous children, remembering and understanding our own experiences of unconscious envy helps in understanding the cause of our offspring's rivalry. How are you engaging with your child? As though they are more fragile? As though they must get out of the way for you to get what you want? Try to change the way you respond to the behaviour in the child, helping them instead to name and connect the uncontrollable feelings inside them with parental empathy to which they can respond. Remember that teenagers are learning to find their own authority. A parent's response to that needs to have its roots in the same soil, rather than seeing the teenager as a rival.

EXPLORE:

- Can you get overly invested and emotional about friendly competition like sport, even if you are not personally involved, e.g. spectating a partner or child?

- As a parent, would you compete with your partner for the attention and affection of your child?
- Do you withdraw and self-exclude rather than claim your portion of the family love?

TIPS:

- Be careful not to overdo the rivalrous touch-line parenting (see box below).
- Teenagers are learning how to deal with self-authority. They are setting you up as the rival. Choose not to accept this role.
- Learn to manage your own jealousies and rather than self-exclude, make sure that you do engage.

Competitiveness in the Workplace – Blue

Your competitive personality can be a real asset in a team, but there may be a tendency to try to excel at the expense of others. There is a risk that you will hold back from hiring other exceptional people for fear of being outdone.

The question to ask is whether your level of competitiveness constantly leaves you feeling alone or with a sense of belonging. If you are able to remain an individual while part of the pack, that can give you a sense of belonging. But if being part of the pack gives you a feeling of being submerged, escape or elimination is the only option to survive. You need to find a different space where it is possible to flourish, but that is lonely because you will miss the pack.

If in the work environment someone is continually leaving the team meeting to use the bathroom at a moment of intense debate, the team is neutered because it needs the participation and agreement of all its members. However, the person will probably feel lonely and will usually return to the group. But the group may no longer trust this person, and may not allocate key roles to them as they see them as someone who is capable of wrecking the team. So again, potential may be self-limiting because certain routes will be closed.

That does not mean that someone with this characteristic may not be successful; on the contrary, they can be hugely successful, but usually only in an environment where consistent interaction with a team is not needed for success – where they can act unilaterally.

A healthy rivalry within a team or with peers is important but the impact of having an over-rivalrous nature can have unintended consequences. It can impact on an individual's ability to hire in good people and to allow their team to flourish.

EXPLORE:

- Do you have a tendency to take on all the work because 'no one else will do it as well'?
- Does your level of competitiveness leave you feeling isolated?

Or,

- Do you hide your driven nature as you worry colleagues will dislike it?

TIPS:

- Don't be afraid to ask for help in hiring people who are close to your own standard.
- Try to compete for a personal best rather than always comparing yourself with another.

- Any tendency towards workaholism could be an invisible form of competitiveness you dare not show in any other way – watch out for this.

Case Study: The Touchline Parent

Over-rivalrous parents may be seen living out their competitive spirit through their children's activities – for example, at school sporting events.

A former county hockey player used to enjoy taking her daughter to the weekly hockey match, shouting encouragement and advice from the sideline. Her daughter seemed to enjoy the game and was pretty good, so her mother was surprised and disappointed when she announced she was giving it up. A few months later, when the season was safely over, the daughter explained that she hadn't given it up at all. She had decided to make her own way to the matches. She could no longer bear to hear her mother screaming advice and tactics to players and the coach.

Resilience

In the face of a significant life event – a bereavement, a job
loss, a family breakdown – are you the person who moves on
so fast it is as if it never happened? Or do you slump into a
space of grievance and collapse, unable to move forward?

Or can you mourn your loss, feel the heartache and yet
find a way through to recovery, finding a new equilibrium
within yourself?

If you are the person who can take the time to mourn, let go of the
old ways to find new ways of growth, and move on, you have resilience; you may have had good early years' attachment, an emotional
bond that connects one person to another across time and space,
allowing that person to also be able to connect with others in a
helpful way. This occurs when the person looking after you allows
you to develop a steady inner core.

Here's another example: a woman is sitting at a table waiting to
be served her lunch in a busy café. The waiter is jostled and pours
hot soup down her arm. With a shriek, the customer tears off her
scalding clothes and pours copious amounts of water over the
injured parts. She insists that the café manager summon an
ambulance to take her to the nearest Accident and Emergency
Department and, despite there being little significant injury, takes
a couple of weeks off work to recover.

Now consider the customer who wipes herself down, notes if
the redness or blistering is serious, and politely declines a kind

bystander's offer of a lift to the hospital. The resilient brain is about our response to a setback or to adverse circumstances. Is our response appropriate? How quickly do we bounce back? The first woman above is demonstrating low resilience.

How well we can recover from a 'fall' – whether that is a cup of scalding coffee over our new suit or tripping on a step in front of a big audience – demonstrates how resilient we are. If you come up with blue on resilience, it might be either that you find it difficult to manage these situations or that you recover immediately without being in touch with the unconscious effect of them. The latter is over-resilience; in this case, it might be that, five years later, your mental 'damaged ankle' crumples under you. This becomes important if we have children. When we mentally fall – for example, when we are having a row with our partner – if we are able to recover and think about what has happened, and learn from it, our children also learn from it. They hear us talking about emotional things. But if the only way to recover is by pretending it never happened, their emotional vocabulary will not be developed.

Although the parent might remain tough, it is quite likely that one child ends up holding the emotion for everyone, and they struggle. If we can mourn the loss of something after a fall – because the person who gets up from a fall is different from the person before the fall – we can adjust to a new way of being in the world. If we lose someone, we can mourn the loss, mourn the change that happens in our own selves because of that loss, and come out the other end. We are a slightly different person, but still authentic. However, if there is not much resilience, we can't let go of the person we were; we do not want to change who we are. That old person is an intrinsic part of us and we can't let go of them. But we all have to become something other, different, and adapt. For teenagers, when their boy- or girlfriends leave them, some recover and some find it really hard because they cannot mourn that part of them that they have lost and become an authentic – but slightly different – person out of the experience. They want to stay the same.

We previously used the example of a speaker arriving at a conference, who falls. If someone has fallen, can they get up, acknowledge the fall, check they are alright, allow others to help, get back into an adult state of mind and carry on heading in the direction they were going in? Or can they take appropriate action if they are not alright, such as go to the hospital? This is good resilience. Lack of resilience is when they fall over and cannot get up again, even if they are fine. They have to take the day/week/ month off work. Over-resilience is when they get up, don't check themselves and don't let anyone help, and they discover three weeks later they have a fractured ankle and have to take three weeks off work.

Where does resilience come from?

Resilience is born in the early years and starts with weaning. Children who have to be weaned in a hurry, unexpectedly, for whatever reason, sometimes feel a deep loss. They may grow up to be either over-resilient, finding coping mechanisms too early to manage their empty feeling of grief, or fragile because they keep seeking something they cannot find and thereby their sense of loss is hard to heal. Sudden weaning is not by any means a terrible thing, there are many other ways of holding a child through it. But if good things constantly get cut off suddenly, as opposed to being reduced slowly and then replaced with something new, it can become difficult. When this is repeated in later life, it will be hard if, as a child, you didn't learn to acknowledge what has happened, incorporate it into yourself, mourn it and move on. Resilience is the ability to grieve and recover.

The resilience domain develops further during the toddler years, when the parent is teaching the young child the appropriate emotional language for response to mishaps. Take, for example, the four-year-old who has been knocked over by a friend and has grazed their elbow. As they sit sobbing on your knee, you comfort and reassure them: 'Gosh, that looks like it must hurt, shall I have a look? Ok, that isn't too bad. I think it shocked you, but Peter didn't mean to bump into you. Shall I help you up and let's check it out together.'

This helps the child to build a vocabulary and emotional response appropriate to their pain.

A young child needs to know that the emotional response they are given matches the reality of the situation. Things start to go awry when the carer continually overreacts, turning small crises into catastrophes and confusing the child with over-emotional vocabulary. Or where they continually under-react, inappropriately brushing off the child's physical and mental pain. When difficult situations arise, the carer needs to take time to explore the circumstances and advise the child on navigating their physical and matching emotional journey. It is the emotional equivalent of teaching a child to cross the road.

At the beginning, we carry them in our arms. Then we cross over with them, holding on to one hand, pointing out the speed of the passing cars. We progress to crossing at their side, within grabbing distance. And then we stand watching anxiously from the pavement. We drill into them, 'Stop, look, listen.' Eventually, however, we let them cross independently.

As the child continues along their developmental journey, they will learn from observing discussions at home around difficult family events. Sometimes there's a tendency to try to protect children, to maintain the fiction that difficulties never arise. But it's far healthier for them to observe and learn the appropriate emotional vocabulary. The over-resilient parents who do not engage in such discussion and who literally just get on with it may not offer their children the same opportunities for learning, and may accidentally form under-resilience in some children rather than pass on their robustness. The child in this no-nonsense household may not learn that it is healthy to acknowledge a problem, and that there may be a necessary adjustment process. The child may feel very alone if no one else appears to be upset or bothered by events that happen and relationships that break. If we lose someone or something, we need to acknowledge and mourn the loss. As commented above, resilience is the ability to grieve and recover, not just to hide from your pain. It will almost certainly come back in another form.

The over-resilience of the 'just get on with it' person is often a façade, masking a fear of the mourning and change that makes up the healthy process of resilience. Events can challenge us, causing physical or emotional pain, and as we respond/adapt, a slightly different version of ourselves emerges from the experience. Those who fear this process of change, who want to stay the same, on a subconscious level refuse to acknowledge that the fall/loss has disrupted things. But this has a habit of working its way out later on in life. The person who trips on the pavement and bounces up, neglecting a broken ankle, is liable to develop problems in their ankle joint later.

Resilience in everyday life

People with green in this characteristic are relatively robust in their ability to bounce back from minor setbacks. They are able to take stock of their internal emotions and assess whether they need to (a) take a deep breath and have a cup of tea, (b) reach out and share with friends/partner, or (c) seek external help. In the event of a more significant trauma, there may be a temporary tendency to descend into a panicky, childlike state, but this is usually followed by a swift recovery to the resting adult state. Later, when the urgency has passed and relief kicks in, there can be a period of oscillation on the ladder: the parent may cope calmly with the childhood emergency in the hospital, but the event can manifest itself after the fact in a strange way. Later, at home, the parent might put the iron in the fridge or the cat in the washing machine.

Greater resilience than usual is necessary to cope with significant life events such as bereavement, separation, parental divorce or job loss. A person who comes out green in this domain will generally have the ability to mourn the circumstance, take themselves off to a safe place and give themselves time to recover. Just as a physical injury requires time to heal, so does an emotional injury. There will be times when help is required from friends, a partner or parents, but also possibly occasions when external help is required from a mentor or counsellor to help regain their normal adult levels of resilience and emotional stability. When this help has been accepted, the person with green resilience is once more back on an even keel.

POINTS TO CONSIDER:

- Encourage communication around any setbacks that arise within the family. Use emotional vocabulary appropriate for the level of the trauma/loss.
- Do you recall as a child the feeling that something bad was going on, but you were being kept out of the loop?

Communicate with children during adverse times, but
guard against overwhelming them with information.
- If you are on your own, remember to seek out others who
may have the emotional language that can respond to
your needs.

Lower levels of resilience are exhibited by those who come up blue
here, where setbacks may provoke a disproportionate or more pro-
longed recovery. In its extreme form, this behaviour can become
habitual and difficult to break: a bad situation arises, the person
suffers emotional trauma, it occurs again, and they begin to find a
comforting normality in the situation. It feels scary to initiate
recovery and easier to give in to the emotional stress. Witness the
couple who break up, can't cope and get back together in a repeti-
tive cycle of stress and distress.

Consider how different the responses are of the green domain
and the blue domain to news of a job redundancy. For the person
who is green here, the loss is acknowledged or cursed, and discussed openly so that the children can think and talk about it too.
It may change family life, sometimes for the better, sometimes for
the worse, but the family swiftly bounces back, moving in a new
direction together, rather than separately. The children learn the
valuable lesson that setbacks can be weathered. By contrast, consider the reaction of the person who is blue. They may panic: 'I
can't cope, we'll have to move house, you'll have to work away from
home. We won't be able to pay for a holiday.' Unfortunately, it is
often the case that the family defaults as a whole to the setting of
the least resilient; everyone has to realign to this fragility.

It is common for the under-resilient to seek out the opposite
attribute in their partner: someone who is capable of putting their
arms around them, both mentally and physically. But they need to

be aware that it is possible for their partner's outward resilience to mask a lack of the true inner security required to weather storms. Think of the archetypal tortured Hollywood superhero, capable of shutting down their own fear under the most dangerous of conditions in order to rescue somebody vulnerable, but who in ordinary life has difficulty with the minor emotional ups and downs of relationships.

Ultimately, with healthy resilience we can allow others to be more or less resilient under certain circumstances. Sometimes we give way, sometimes we are the stronger one – there is no extreme of always giving way or never giving way. It is all about how we manage fear, anger, anxiety or weakness (the fall) without shutting others out.

Case Study: The Descent into Panic

A surgeon used to dealing with life-and-death decisions describes her panic when her young child had a convulsion and she tried to call an ambulance. She repeatedly jabbed at the buttons on her phone, but couldn't get through. Her friend gently took the phone from her and dialled 999. Rather than 998.

While capable of extreme resilience in dealing with her patients in the work environment, when it was her own child whose life was in danger, the mother descended to the bottom rung of the ladder in a heartbeat.

If you code green for resilience

You are a naturally resilient person. You can bounce back from a crisis and you are a dependable person to have around in a tricky situation. You have a strong ability to adapt to stress, but you need to be aware that you will not be able to cope with an unlimited amount of adversity. Try to learn to heed your own internal emotional barometer and to develop strategies for the safe space and safe time you will require when your own emotional healing is necessary.

You are able to look inside, assess your state of mind and find the internal resources you need to stay well and happy. The green resilient brain can wake up each morning and, whether they feel good or bad, they can think through what is needed to regulate their emotional temperature – whether that is a cup of coffee, a chat to a friend or a visit to the hospital.

Resilience in Relationships – Green
In an established relationship, it is your combined resilience that counts. Even if you are both naturally resilient, there are times – sometimes concurrent, sometimes not – when each of you will be running on empty. You have the capacity to support your partner and friendship group through their own ups and downs. You have broad enough shoulders to partner with others less resilient than yourself.

EXPLORE:

- How often do you reach out to others for support?
- Do you notice when others are less resilient?
- Does your natural sense of balance stop your more 'poetic' side from being explored?

TIPS:

- Learn to recognise when combined resilience is being stretched. Talk, listen, take a break.
- Remember, it is your combined resilience that counts – don't forget to watch out for when others need a shoulder.
- Moderation does not allow for much passion – let this in sometimes.

Resilience in the Family – Green

Because you are resilient yourself, you will set a good example to your children or other members of your family about how they can grow to be balanced in this domain. You will be a comfort to children, parents or siblings when they need help. You will tend to adopt the role of the bedrock that supports everyone else, but remind yourself that the weight you yourself can support is not infinite.

Remember that resilience can be age-related. Adolescents and those in their twenties are often at the peak of their physical and mental prowess and thus generally more resilient; at this age they need to be able to recover quickly and start to rebuild. Thus it is no accident that most successful survivors of disasters are within this age group – young teenagers are often still too fragile, while those in their thirties are old enough to sometimes lose the will to continue. We become more nervous and risk averse as we get older, partly because our capacity to empathise is not fully developed until our mid- to late twenties. With the exception of those who are not very well, most young people want to push on and move on, and have the adaptability to forge a new life out of the rubble.

EXPLORE:

- Think about your family – where are they on the resilience scale?
- How much does your family's ups and downs affect you?
- Do you truly listen to your own emotional self?

TIPS:

- Watch out for those who are less resilient than you. You may find it easy to self-adjust, but others in your family might need more communication.
- Be careful when you are among a lot of less-resilient people – even green domains can buckle under too much pressure. Watch out for being the last one standing.
- Plan ahead to support the less resilient in predictable life events, e.g. moving house, a new job, leaving home.

Resilience in the Workplace – Green

You have the bounce-back factor. You can adapt to stressful work situations and recover well from any setbacks. Your resilience makes you a valued team member and your support of others in the work setting will be much appreciated. You can navigate tough issues without help. Nevertheless, when necessary, you are able to ask for and accept appropriate help.

EXPLORE:

- Do you recognise your resilience?
- Do you make the most of it and push yourself? Are you being sufficiently stretched?
- Are you sensitive enough to those in your workplace who are less resilient?

TIPS:

- Notice that this is a real gift for you and for those around you.
- Don't be afraid to push yourself forward for different/ challenging jobs or promotions.
- Be alert to impending crises in colleagues and employees. Encourage the use of appropriate channels for stress management and counselling.

If you code blue for resilience

At times, you'll take longer than usual to bounce back from life's traumas. With insight into your vulnerability, you can work towards improving your wellbeing. Remember that this brain characteristic may make you sympathetic towards other people with similar vulnerabilities. It is possible that you have significant insight and that you mask your vulnerability well in some aspects of your life. Be careful not to overdo this, as it may take its toll.

Some people are so tough that they seem to live in survival mode, emotionally shutting down just to survive. If you are this tough, it's hard for others to know what you're feeling, hard for them to connect with you. At the other extreme, you may wake up every morning wondering if you will make it through the day. Somewhere within you, you haven't formed a healthy internal parent, the bit of yourself that helps you through the day. Try talking to yourself – kindly. Try not to catastrophise. Aim for a steadier state of mind where you can acknowledge, without collapsing, that someone else can let you down, and where you can think about looking after yourself. Begin to take your own emotional temperature and try to bring it back to normal.

Taking an acceptable risk to move forward to an output is healthy resilience. So, the risk involved in crossing the road to get a pint of milk is acceptable; crossing the road to buy the milk and playing chicken in the traffic on the way is getting a kick out of playing with the dangers of the road. Where the pleasure is in the danger, this indicates an internal lack of healthy resilience because you have to flirt with danger in order to feel alive.

The converse can also be true: for some, the ordinary risk of crossing the road has become so great in their mind that they cannot step outside the door for fear that they or someone else might die in the endeavour. This agoraphobic state of mind is closely related to resilience. This need to take risks or take no risks can play out in everything from relationships to alcohol and drugs.

If you are obsessively tidy or obsessively messy, it tells you something about your resilience. You will remember we talked about our 'internal scaffolding' in the introduction. People with OCD have to build external scaffolding because they struggle to create an internal framework. As we mentioned earlier, people who are totally chaotic in the environment around them usually have chaotic internal worlds and are trying to make their internal and external worlds match. Otherwise they don't feel that they fit in, and so they are allowing their lack of internal scaffolding to rule their external world.

Resilience in Relationships – Blue
Although you might cope well with many of the ups and downs of everyday life together, you may tend to go to pieces with more significant difficulties. You will thrive with the support of a partner or friends with a higher level of resilience.

EXPLORE:

- Do you self-identify as someone who struggles with life's ups and downs?
- Are your relationships and friendships easily derailed when you hit a problem?

Or,

- Are you so over-resilient and tough that no one can connect with you when you are in survival mode?

TIPS:

- Learn to be upfront with your partner about your relative lack of resilience, but don't make it an excuse.
- Stay closely in touch with your internal emotional barometer. Develop strategies for safe space and healing time.
- In a relationship, over-resilience and shutting down can feel to the other person like being shut out.

Resilience in the Family – Blue

There will be occasions when you need increased support from those around you. But you will also have a lot of insight that can be used to positive effect in supporting other, similarly less-resilient family members. Your experience of feeling out of your depth may at times allow you to empathise with others going through such an experience themselves.

EXPLORE:

- Do you overburden younger family members when you are going through difficult times?

- Do you overreact when your children have a minor accident?

Or,

- Do you believe you can weather anything, however hard, so much so that you are unreachable?

TIPS:

- Aim to develop a support network outside of the family, to whom you can turn when times are tough.
- See if you can get your emotional language to match the reality of the situation.
- Notice that you might be shutting down on your own legitimate reactions to pain and therefore responding inappropriately.

Resilience in the Workplace – Blue

You find it difficult to bounce back when hit by issues. A serious setback can affect you considerably, and you may need time and support in order to recover. Many work environments are becoming more understanding and supportive of colleagues in difficulty, so it can now be easier to be more open about these needs.

Resilient people are often thought of as being tough, but tough people are not necessarily resilient in everyday life. They may have had to build external scaffolding to be super-tough on the outside to hold their internal scaffolding steady. People who have been born and bred with their own internal scaffolding can adapt – it doesn't matter what is around them, they can move with it.

EXPLORE:

- Do you bring your life crises into the workplace? More so than other colleagues?
- Are you aware of the support networks available at work?

Or,

- Do you never miss a day, even if there is a bereavement close to home?

TIPS:

- Where possible, try to choose a supportive environment.
- In the event of a real crisis, aim to be open with colleagues. They might be more understanding than you think. Let them see your willingness to make use of the wellbeing tools on offer.
- Develop your own toolkit, a set of interventions or behaviours that you can adapt when you realise you are under-reacting in a crisis. Ask a mentor, friend or coach to help.

Independence

*Are you overly self-sufficient, never asking for help
because you worry deeply about looking small or losing
your independence? Do you believe that if there is a problem
in a project and you take it back to do yourself, it will work
faultlessly? Do you hide any hint of need or desire because
you fear it will lead to being taken over? Are you so tough
that you live in survival mode, emotionally shutting down
just to get by?*

*Or do you know when there are some times that you want
help or intimate companionship and some times that you
do not?*

Consider this scenario: a young girl is unwell and her parent takes
her to hospital, bringing along an older sibling. The sick child is
admitted, but the older child is afraid of hospitals and doesn't want
to stay overnight. So the parent phones around for help, and a kind
friend offers to take care of the older sibling overnight.

There is a second parent in the same situation. Even though the
parent knows that the older sibling needs to go home, they request
an extra mattress on the floor of the hospital room so that all three
of them can stay in the hospital together overnight. It doesn't cross
this parent's mind to phone round friends for help.

Here, then, is an overly independent person, one who is unable
to put the wishes of an anxious child over their own fear of appear-
ing to need help. They cannot make calls to friends and family to

help out because, in their mind, that would mean implicitly admitting a weakness in the system. They may believe they are doing the right thing by not intruding on another, not showing that anyone else is needed, because in their view that would be a diminishing experience. They believe it is ok for someone else to call people for help, and are not consciously judgemental of them, but, somewhere deep in the recesses of their mind, those who called for help would have been put into a box labelled 'Weak'. The overly independent person cannot see that asking a favour is a normal and ordinary thing to do – that people don't usually mind helping, that it can be reciprocal, even an interactive pleasure. This extreme independence can become withholding and punitive, and people on the other end of it often feel they are not allowed to do what they do best. And the result can be the independent person not behaving responsibly on behalf of themselves and others, including their own children.

Where does independence come from?

As a child grows, they progress from the total dependency of infancy to the relative independence of adulthood. We all have to detach from the umbilical cord when we are born and learn to reattach progressively to our physical nutritional life-support systems. Likewise, our emotional attachment must undergo similar change. We are attached in a healthy way if we are enabled to step out and be curious about our environment and come back to safety when we are frightened, overwhelmed or tired. At each stage of development we can tolerate a little more independence, emerging from behind our parental shield. For those who are not given this opportunity and are either allowed to go too far or are left too long when feeling overwhelmed, or those who are given the message that the world is too dangerous and are over-shielded, healthy attachment – and detachment – is harder to achieve and maintain.

A steady progression along this pathway results in an adult with a healthy mix of self-sufficiency and independence. So the green side of this characteristic has a balanced amount of neediness and desire to be looked after, attachment with a capacity to connect to another, and enough interdependence to be healthy.

The blue side of this characteristic comes about when the element of need for others is relatively suppressed; for example, as a result of perceived abandonment, particularly in the first three years of infancy. At this age, we all have a very deep, infant-like belief that we will not survive if we are left alone. This is so frightening that we may force ourselves to learn to survive alone. Thereafter, we find it difficult to act otherwise. We engage less with the usual ebb and flow of aloneness and togetherness that is part of the normal pattern of life. Most people are able to form close attachments with others, understanding that this carries with it the risk of the loss of that person, but that the loss will be survivable after a period of grief. The overly independent person worries that such a loss would not be survivable; they make a subconscious choice not to expose themselves to the risk, a choice which manifests as self-sufficiency.

With the more balanced independence of a green state of mind, there is the ability to function autonomously, and to return and attach. There is a good understanding of the requirement to interact with other human beings. The blue side, however, comes from a fear that you could actually destroy a relationship through your need. In your desire to attach to someone, you fear becoming so jealous of their time that you will not survive. Moreover, your partner will not survive being with you because you are too needy and too unworthy of being with them. You also believe others will be envious of your attachment to them.

The normal human desire for dependency is thus squashed down so far that you become incredibly self-sufficient, to the extent where you don't really believe you need anyone else – making a virtue of necessity. It looks incredibly independent, but those who are really independent have a good old-fashioned bit of neediness and an understanding that they do require other human beings to attach to, feed, pick up and so on.

For much of life, independence may appear to be a positive driving force, allowing the blue domain to drive on through situations where others might hesitate. The university student described in the case study might appear at first glance to be someone who is committed and steadfast. However, underneath, she may have been forged from less robust elements – fear of attaching, fear of loss if the attachment disappears, fear of struggling with that loss. To prevent any of this happening, the independent person tends to push people away, worried that if they do merge with someone and they lose that person, they will be devastated by the loss.

Independence in everyday life

The independent child may appear self-sufficient and appealing: they can travel freely and do interesting things, managing without anyone's help, unable to see why others are floored by what they consider to be irrelevancies. But sometimes, as they become older, others may question this strong level of self-sufficiency and independence. The flipside of this independence is that often the child's normal level of neediness has been crushed and unconsciously pushed right down. They subconsciously believe that if they don't push away their neediness and desire to be loved, they will never be able to let go of the person showing them that care, they will simply remain desperately wanting something they can't be given.

In family life, the independent person manifests as an interesting mix. They may be loyal and unlikely to betray those closest to them, but at the same time they are not really bothered by saying, 'I've had enough of this now, I'm off.' This generates a degree of internal conflict, which tends to be managed and justified by a walk-in/walk-out cycle. So, the independent person will walk out and do something that suits them, then their loyalty will kick in and they will come back for a while and participate in some family-/relationship-based activity. After a while, that will be too much for them, so they will walk off to do something entirely self-related, before loyalty and guilt send them rushing back. This pattern can play out as large amounts of time at work (late nights, weekends, etc.), alternating with guilt-driven, over-the-top family holidays. However, it can also sometimes be harnessed usefully in jobs which lend themselves to an intense on-off cycle.

Expression of the over-independent characteristic tends to diminish with age, an occurrence that may on occasion contribute to the classic 'mid-life crisis'. People may have married but are workaholics, spending an inordinate amount of time in their workspace, not necessarily with their team – it is often them and their client, or them and their paperwork. Then, at some point, perhaps as they head towards the death of their parents or a similar emotional crisis, their self-sufficiency starts to break down and they walk into a mid-life crisis. Even if they are in the perfect marriage and they are not having relationship problems, they can feel desperately alone. They have effectively made themselves alone by excluding themselves from family life. Although they are very loyal to individuals, at the end of the day they are self-sufficient and do what they need to do for themselves, to stay away from their own internal pain, loss of youth or other fears. The obvious answer is to seek help, but of course that is precisely what they find hardest to do. Sometimes the answer is for someone to seek help privately first, rather than too publicly.

The softening of this independent characteristic has led to many a happy late marriage. Sometimes these couples marry very quietly and do not invite many people to the ceremony. They haven't made much of their relationship before the wedding, and are slightly shy about admitting the possibility that they might not actually want to be the life-long soloists they swore they were.

The couple don't realise that there may be a fallout from this. After the ceremony, there might be a flurry of furious communications along the lines of: 'I would have been at the church for you, why didn't you tell me?' Response: 'We thought you might think it was an imposition, or think differently about us when we have always appeared so independent.' Reply: 'It's amazing and we would always want to be there for you at times of importance to you.' There can be a whole mess of fears and assumptions coming into play about what other people might think, but often the attempt to read their minds and avoid comment is actually way off course. More people than you think might want to benignly support rather than judge your choices.

POINTS TO CONSIDER:

- Do you recall from your own childhood any traumatic episodes of perceived abandonment? Could it have been dealt with better, e.g. with greater communication ahead of time?
- For some, healthy trust in others comes easily. Some find their experiences have left them trying to second-guess others' motivation. It can be worth considering where you are on this spectrum.

- Teenage behaviour may fluctuate alarmingly between clinginess and detachment. Don't be alarmed; this represents the final throes in transition from childhood to adult independence.

If you code green for independence

Your self-sufficiency is balanced with a healthy understanding of the benefits of companionship and connection with your fellow human beings. Sometimes you want help or intimate companionship, sometimes not. Your desires and needs can exist without overwhelming your own space. You might lose this equanimity when times are rough – in grief, for example – but you will find your balance again.

Independence in Relationships – Green
You are comfortable staying at home while your partner or flatmate goes out, but equally you enjoy and value evenings out in company. You seek advice from partners and friends, and you enjoy their support in making decisions.

EXPLORE:

- Do you generally know when you need to lean on friends and when you can work it out for yourself?
- Does it feel like others in your household seek your opinion less than you seek theirs?
- Have you experienced partners who are a little more detached or less aware?

TIPS:

- You are probably quick at assimilating yours and others' judgements – sometimes you could give others some breathing space to catch up with you on this.
- You may need to remember that other people have more inner fears and worries about what others think than you do. Understanding this may lower the tension.
- If you recognise that a friend or partner is blue in this domain, you will need to respect their barriers and boundaries in the early stages of the relationship. Be patient in allowing emotional intimacy to grow.

Independence in the Family – Green

The home dynamic benefits from your inclusivity around family decisions. You understand that children feel important and included when asked for their thoughts in an age-appropriate way.

EXPLORE:

- Can you generally acknowledge your desires and needs and exist without overwhelming your own space?
- Do you notice how good you are by yourself and when the family is around?
- It is worth thinking back to how you have managed more difficult periods of life.
- You might lose your equanimity when times are rough, but don't lose sight of the fact that you will find your balance again.

TIPS:

- Watch out for when your children leave home – you might need to find a more creative outlet for your capacity for inclusive thinking.
- Emotional balance comes easily to you, but looking back at your own life might help you to understand those who find it less straightforward.

Independence in the Workplace – Green

You are a natural team player and judge well when to put yourself, others or the organisation first. You demonstrate empathy with others and can spot when to offer support. Equally, you are comfortable asking for help yourself when necessary.

EXPLORE:

- Do you find it easy to make friends in the workplace?
- Do you show independence of action appropriate to your job description and your level of experience?
- Do you enjoy collaborative ventures?

TIPS:

- It is in your nature to want everyone to find reconciliation easy. You may need to learn to live with the fact that others can't always do this.
- There may be times, if you are seeking promotion, when you will need to take a little more risk than you would like. Have a think about what this might look like.
- Be aware that promotion to management sometimes loses this peer-group community. You may have to seek help to be in leadership.

Case Study: The Unsympathetic University Student

Sophie was a university student completing her final-year dissertation. She describes being bemused when one of her fellow students confessed to struggling to focus on her own dissertation because a friend of theirs had suddenly decided to leave the university. Sophie recalls that her reaction was to think, 'Just get on with it. What does our friend's decision have to do with us sitting down at night to write our dissertations?' Sophie could not understand that changes such as this might rock the boat and that her fellow student regarded the departure of their friend as a significant loss, which unsettled her.

If you code blue for independence

For you, it tends to be a case of, 'My way or the highway.' This does not mean that you are inherently selfish, but that you have an innate tendency to disregard the views of others. You may well be very generous in supporting others when they ask for help, but you will find it difficult to ask for support and help for yourself.

On the plus side, self-sufficiency can be an appealing characteristic, and can allow for strength during difficult times in life and work. You can be trusted not to follow the herd. Once your trust is won, you are capable of immense loyalty.

Independence in Relationships – Blue

You have a subconscious fear of attachment and, in the initial stage of relationships, you may put up barriers. Hopefully, you will align yourself with someone willing to respect barriers and boundaries in these early stages. Be aware that you will not come across as needy (even though this is your deepest-rooted fear), but rather as somewhat aloof or detached. It will take a long time for you to allow someone to get under your skin, but you have the potential to become a very loyal partner.

People with blue in this domain who end up feeling terribly alone may prefer to seek help secretly rather than publicly. For them, information cannot be shared because there is a fear that other people will use it against them. Even something fun cannot be shared – for example, if they are having a new bathroom installed. Someone might say it should be pink when you want it green – then what do you do? You are loyal and may want to allay their judgement of you, but also don't want anyone else intruding. So you don't share any details until everything is set in stone, then you can say, 'Come and look at my new bathroom!' If you can't share the journey, it may be best to 'seek help secretly' – not because that is a good thing, but because it is the only way you are going to get help, and you need to move forward acknowledging your own limitations.

EXPLORE:

- Do you have a lack of desire to 'couple', and prefer to go it alone? Can your independence feel like emotional coldness to others?
- Do you have the new bathroom installed without discussing the colour with your partner or flatmate?

Or,

- Do you never dare make an independent decision?

TIPS:

- Recognise that you might be afraid of having your independence compromised. Can you persuade yourself to take that risk, reminding yourself that it might bring you more than you lose?
- You might be terrified that your voice won't be heard in a household decision. Trusting people is hard; you need practice.
- You may fear the other person will lose regard for you if you disagree with them. Pick someone safe and try sharing something small to see if it can be tolerated. It can be something as minor as what colour top you should buy. Don't pick someone who is doomed to want to control – actively seek out someone really likely to give you your head.

Case Study: The Complicated Business of Choosing Clothes

Mo is an independent type. He always selects his wardrobe without discussion with his husband David, but tonight it is their wedding anniversary dinner and he would like to make sure that the occasion is special. He asks David's advice on choosing which shirt to wear: 'White or blue?' he says, as he holds them up.

David knows that Mo rarely ever wears white as he thinks it makes him look washed out. 'Well, the blue is really striking,' he says. So Mo wears the blue. They have a good evening. And with luck Mo has not been put off seeking advice again in the future.

Independence in the Family – Blue

You have a tendency to disregard the wishes of other family members and, as a result, at times you may be perceived as controlling. You are missing out on the support and fun to be derived from the family discussion. There is a risk that you end up feeling isolated or excluded from the wider family.

Remember that children need their parents to help them voice difficult emotions, such as envy and jealousy, around their siblings. Voicing a child's envy for them is very helpful because it makes it conscious and takes the power and conflict out of it. But, to do that for a child, we need to know that it is in ourselves also. It is an age-old pattern – work out the feeling in ourselves, voice the feeling for our children (or other family members), make it conscious, take the power away, diminish the conflict.

Sometimes people with blue here will say they have had the perfect upbringing. It's a kind of defence. No upbringing is perfect but there is often a reluctance to talk about it – they have few memories. They just think it was all fine. Notice if you can't engage in your own childhood narrative – that might be worth thinking about. We often hear people say, 'My mum was great at cooking but she was rubbish at sitting on the floor and playing,' or, 'Dad was hopeless, he never came to any of my football matches, but he could really build some great Lego with me.' It's a normal good/bad mix. If you hear yourself saying, 'It was all perfect, it was all fine,' and you can't unravel the ordinary good bits and ordinary not-so-good bits, with no narrative around those parental ups and downs, that is really worth noticing. Part of it is being loyal – you cannot betray your family and daren't even consider that one or other of your parents was not good at something. Think about how you understand your family of origin (i.e., those with whom you grew up from very young) and how that helps you to find different ways of having good attachments to others.

EXPLORE:

- Do you find it difficult to imagine another person's point of view? Do you tend to disregard it?
- Do your children, parents or siblings complain that you don't involve them in decisions?

Or,

- Do you let everyone else have their own way because it is so much easier than the possibility of having your own views rejected?

TIPS:

- Aim to encourage those close to you to tell you when they feel dismissed, so that you can appreciate how others experience you.
- Notice that making decisions on your own may be your way of protecting yourself from being dismissed by others. Try practising in a safe forum with people you trust.
- If you can learn that occasional rejection within relationships is not catastrophic, you may be able to engage more often.

Independence in the Workplace – Blue

You work better independently and flourish when giving advice or consultation. Your single-mindedness and determination can be put to great advantage if you are allowed to work independently or in an 'expert' capacity. You are likely to be quite risk-happy and entrepreneurial in your approach, due to a lack of concern for the views or needs of others or the requirement for feedback and affirmation.

You are probably very good when dealing with clients or in other 'front-facing' roles that require composure, discretion and independence. Freelance or portfolio careers may carry appeal. You may derive less enjoyment in an environment where there is a very strong conformist culture and where all employees are expected to put the organisation first.

In work terms this can also play out with someone spending huge amounts of time at work until guilt kicks in, so they have a huge family holiday. Then guilt kicks in again and they go back to work and work weekends as well. And so on. There are many jobs that lend themselves to that all-or-nothing cycle.

A common characteristic for people with blue here is a denial that anyone can help them. It can stem from them trying to work out whether, if they allow someone to have input into their thinking, the other will steal it from them. This can make collaboration much more complicated – the independent person cannot show the world that anything came from anyone else. It breaks their fantasy of being independent and self-sufficient. This person can be a wonderfully directive boss, but may be less able to collaborate on an equal footing.

Consider the employee in a big city firm who is really struggling. The firm is offering them legitimate help but the employee's response is, 'If I take this help, the firm will think I am weak and will want to get rid of me.' In fact the firm is saying, 'We're not that awful, we're actually quite benign, and if you show that you can take help, we will do everything we can to keep you. But if you are really stubborn and don't take the help, we won't be able to contain your difficulty.' Because the employee is self-sufficient to the nth degree, it is not possible for them to hear the help. All they hear is that the firm will think they are weak if they say yes, and will throw them out, because secretly they believe it is a test. Somewhere in their past there is a non-benign authority who has threatened them in some way if they show weakness, and that is a very hard thing from which to escape.

Those with blue in this domain tend to be entrepreneurial or work for someone who is. Some become stay-at-home parents where they have a lot of control over their own environment. They may become quite powerful in this role and their partner may feel a bit excluded. Remember that collaborating is a very powerful driver of upward progression and growth. In the beginning, an independent person will tend to rise quickly because they are self-sufficient, they are able to do things, they are not needy of their bosses. However, then it plateaus because suddenly being self-sufficient is not such a good thing. People start to see that the overly independent are not team players, they are not joining forces to create new things. There are limitations as to what can be created without another person putting something into it. So a sharp promotion, quick growth and praise are often achieved early, but then somewhere along the way it plateaus off badly, and often the overly independent person does not understand why.

EXPLORE:

- Do your colleagues regard you as unapproachable?
- How do you respond when your view is challenged? Do you enjoy the debate? Or close it down?

Or,

- Do you never challenge another in case they squash you?

TIPS:

- Work on asking for support from others to stop you becoming too isolated. Even if you do not think you need help, try asking for it anyway.
- Although it may seem as though independence is the only way, try to incorporate consulting others as a normal part of your working life. It may not come naturally to you.
- Pick someone grounded and reliable and try sharing a decision. Don't pick someone who is equally independent.
- Learning to collaborate is the way to get on in your career, and your underlying fear of showing neediness, fear of being envied and of envying others needs to be addressed. Find a way to believe that it is not weak or dangerous to share.

Perfectionist

Do you believe that you or someone else will attack anything you produce that is less than perfect? Do you believe that you cannot produce anything at all? Or that anything you do produce will be damaged, or will fail through your own neglect or incompetence, or the attacks of others?

Or do you believe you can create something that, with the help of others, can change and grow, and improve?

Does anything in the following scene strike a chord? One partner is assembling flat-pack furniture in the bedroom. The other partner is downstairs when they hear a crash, a clatter of tools on the floor and much swearing. Fearing injury, they run upstairs. What they say is, 'What happened? Are you alright?' What their partner hears is, 'You are incompetent. You can't even put furniture together without hurting yourself.' The assembler says something like, 'This thing slipped and broke in my hands. It's your fault for buying such cheap furniture. Why are you so stingy?'

Welcome to the perfectionist domain, which is all about our sensitivity to criticism, our inability to acknowledge our mistakes and our tendency to blame others for them. This is the childlike, binary world of blame and not-blame, where omnipotence is passed from the child to the adult, who drops the ball. As adults, it is very difficult to recognise this in ourselves.

The perfectionist cannot be seen to be less than perfect; something in them works really hard all the time to have the moral high ground. They are always watching out to make sure that the people who matter to them do not see their flaws. They have a completely unconscious drive to ensure that nothing they do can be criticised. At heart, the driving force is not so much to look perfect but to be uncriticisable. Perfectionists are incredibly sensitive to criticism of any sort, including the benign, caring kind which is based on genuine concern about what might be going on. Offers of help are often misconstrued as criticism.

Where does perfectionism come from?

The perfectionist domain is linked to a child's ability to take responsibility for their actions. It is moulded by early experiences of being blamed for mistakes – sometimes their own and sometimes those of another.

Consider the situation: a four-year-old boy drops a cup right in front of you. In all likelihood, the child will immediately declare, 'It wasn't me!' Now, you know it was him, and he knows it was him; the fib is obvious. It is normal for all children to explore the difference between truth and lies, to deceive on occasions when trouble is brewing and to need help to understand this approach. If the cup smashes, a parent might react in many ways: a yell, sympathetic understanding or overly patient frustration, but then the child will be forgiven with a hug and the event blows over. Every now and again, however, if the accident catches the parent at a stressful moment, the response may be angrier, and reduce the child to tears. When next the child breaks something, he is very likely to think, 'Well, I know how much trouble I am going to get into now, so instead of saying anything, I will hide the broken bits under a cushion. It will be as if it never happened!' A very normal behaviour pattern, played out in every household.

A problem might develop, however, when a parent responds repeatedly to each and every mistake in an angry or intimidating manner. Often it is not so much what is said, but the manner in which it is said. A child will grow up overly scared of the consequences of their actions. The child might subconsciously act as if, 'I won't get told off if I behave perfectly', or 'I won't get told off if I'm not caught out'. They are remarkably similar; one is the action of not getting caught, the other is a mind that develops a self that is part hidden, as no one can be perfect. This thought pattern is perpetuated into adulthood.

We can see a similar pattern when the toddler bounces up from falling over or making a mistake and struts around for a little while, pretending all is well and showing off (this is the coping strategy). After a little while, their unconscious and their conscious heads catch up with each other and they tire. They want to be caught by the adult and comforted without feeling abandoned or made to feel even smaller. They are on a rollercoaster of feeling 'I'm big – no, I'm little'.

Perhaps the parent doesn't pick up the toddler, catch them, kiss them, put them to bed and say 'I love you', but instead leaves them running around, showing off until they are overtired, then yells at them. Perhaps the parent thinks it is kind to let them play it out – often because they identify strongly with the child. Their own experience may have left them feeling that they were always stopped from doing something midway through and they felt powerless amidst the adults, but they, in this case, may be overcompensating when their child is still at an age to need a parent to catch them. If the power and the responsibility are appropriately assumed by the parent, the child is relieved of that weight. Safety then kicks in, and all is right with the world.

But if the parent doesn't do that, it becomes a negotiation and the child suddenly doesn't feel safe. Their fantasy of being 'big' overwhelms them. If a child is made to feel inappropriately big, when they go out into the world, and discovers they are not as big as they believe, their unconscious age is inappropriate and they feel very unsafe. The parent has not been able to grab the unconscious age of the child and line it up with their actual age. Of course, we know as adults that parents do not control the world, but the toddler believes it is in a parent's power to do so and they are kept safe in that belief. The reason for this is that the baby and toddler believe they have power over the parents – they scream, parents come running. This gives them a sense of omnipotence, and therefore reassures them of their own survival. Safety at this stage depends on there being no shades of grey, and if that internal safety looks grey, that is catastrophic. That sense of omnipotence is assumed to exist in the key carers, and so is transferred from baby/toddler to adult. This transitions in the child at around seven years old, when the child is no longer so dependent on the power of the adult; their realisation that adults are separate and not as omnipotent as believed and the world is not black and white is not so catastrophic.

The idea that someone is big and can solve things and someone is small and without a voice often stays with us throughout life. The rollercoaster of feeling competent and in control or diminished and powerless is something many of us have to manage on a daily basis. The possibility that cups get broken by children and adults and 'stuff happens' and there isn't always someone to legitimately blame is a fairly sophisticated concept in developmental terms. We all look for the fault behind things going wrong, whether it is the company that made the bad furniture, as in our flat-pack example, or the government behind the company that didn't regulate the standards sufficiently. The perfectionist can never be seen to drop a plate, real or metaphorical. If someone else tries helpfully to advise on carrying plates safely or to commiserate over broken shards benignly, the perfectionist will hear only criticism and blame, and withdraw. They will try to hide any broken fragments or mistakes in all aspects of their life.

POINTS TO CONSIDER:

- Do you recall your parents/guardians being overly strict about minor misdemeanours? Do you think this has affected your present state of mind in response to things going wrong?
- Be aware of the negative effects of excessive criticism. Remember, it is often the tone of delivery rather than just the content of the message that lands on the other person that matters.
- Teach children clearly and consistently that taking responsibility is always the best policy. Reward them for honesty in admitting mistakes. Do you do the same?

Perfectionism in everyday life

The perfectionist characteristic is built on a subconscious need to appear perfect at all times and in all circumstances. Work does not so much need to look perfect, but to be uncriticisable. There is hyper-sensitivity to criticism of any kind, including even the benign, caring concern of friends and family. This is one of the brain markers where it is very rare for us to have insight into our own perfectionist tendencies.

Many of us feel inadequate from time to time, fearing that we may be found wanting in some respect. Perhaps we are not good enough as a housekeeper or provider, or attractive enough or clever enough in our own eyes. We develop coping mechanisms to make ourselves appear adequate, and to avoid the humiliation of being found out. The most common mechanism is hiding, as, for example, in the case of a student who cannot show the draft of an essay but only the perfect final outcome. Because the draft cannot be discussed and encouraged to develop, there is no potential for growth. Fear of 'being found out' may cut off the whole essay. Some PhDs remain unfinished because of this characteristic. In the long term, the requirement and excuses for continual hiding can become increasingly wearing and paralysing.

An alternative coping mechanism is that of disowning goals once we have failed to achieve them. For example, a teenager who fails to get into a particular university may then demean the college/course instead of venting their disappointment and moving on. When they have failed to get into College X, we hear, 'Well, actually I really wanted to go to Y or Z anyway, because College X doesn't do my subject very well!' The narrative is retold, and the failure is never properly acknowledged and learned from. While it's undoubtedly a gift to like what you can have in life, the emotional literacy of the person who diminishes what they can't have may be curbed. Disappointment is never really felt and the joy of the place that is received isn't truly given space.

Someone with the perfectionist brain may be trying to do something that they believe is more perfect than it really is, and if someone else benignly tries to add to it or improve it, they will draw back. The perfectionist lacks insight into the fact that their habit of hiding mistakes may cause alarm in others. At work, they cannot understand why they are passed over for promotion. Why were they, who have done things perfectly, not chosen over the other person who made twenty-six mistakes? They do not realise that the company is more concerned by their lack of maturity than the number of mistakes they may make. This can cause great resentment in an employee.

Case Study: The Teacher with the Disruptive Student

Ian sought therapy because, amongst other things, he was struggling to progress in his career as a teacher. He described an occasion on which a student in the class had erupted in anger, shouting loudly. The deputy headmaster had been passing and knocked at the door. 'Are you alright?' he asked. Ian answered that he was fine and went on to explain why the student was yelling. However, he felt mortified by the event, interpreting the intervention as, 'Can't you control your class? What mistake have you made to result in the children shouting at you?'

With some self-exploration, however, Ian conceded that the deputy headmaster was generally a caring individual, and that his query may have been empathetic rather than judgemental: 'This class is always difficult. I've been there too. Are you alright?'

It may take some time for a boss to recognise that someone is blue in this domain, as superficial appearances may be of a mature and fully-functioning professional. However, the risks may be considerable. If the blue perfectionist is working in a finance company, he may potentially be unable to tell the boss when something is amiss with his figures, even though the error may be genuine, with no intention to defraud. There are many well-known examples where the concealment of errors within financial institutions has contributed to economic disaster (see Case Study: Rogue Trader, below). Potentially even more catastrophic is the blue perfectionist health-care worker who might fail to acknowledge an error that has occurred in the treatment of their patients. Or the pharmaceutical company worker who fails to acknowledge a potential problem with a drug. It's a form of shame. We are no longer able to calculate the consequences and we become childlike. Our mind unconsciously propels us into the place of shame and humiliation and we will then do anything to avoid feeling this way.

Case Study: Rogue Trader

The potentially disastrous effect of not owning up to errors is well illustrated by the story of a trader with Barings Bank in the 1990s. Using 'error accounts' to hide losses from his bosses, he continued to make increasingly risky trades with huge amounts of money in an attempt to recoup his losses. His behaviour eventually culminated in debts of £827 million, and the collapse of Britain's oldest merchant bank.

On the other hand, in different circumstances, a blue-brained perfectionist can become an extremely thorough worker, careful about crossing t's and dotting i's in an effort to avoid making mistakes. They may thrive in a job where the work is fact-and-figure-based, with reconciliation columns, and the responsibility for decision-making is limited.

In relationship terms, it can be extremely difficult for two perfectionist brains to co-exist harmoniously. The partners will both have a tendency to regress to the position of the toddler in the dynamic, and the relationship can become an emotional rollercoaster. In sexual terms, it can be difficult to find a point at which both partners can be consenting adults at the same time, and frequency of intimacy may tail off. Partners in this situation may drift apart and seek solace in new relationships, where their vulnerability has not yet been noticed and where they are safe from criticism. However, unless they have matured so that the relationship with the second partner is different, the relief is short-lived. As the new couple take on the responsibilities that go along with a longer-term relationship, they may end up in the same loop.

If you code green for perfectionism

A green perfectionist code may sound like a contradiction but it means you are someone who naturally wants a good outcome in any given situation, but who can also share an unfinished version and tolerate imperfections. Green here indicates that you are upfront, open and honest about mistakes. You are strong enough to accept the consequences of your actions and do not blame others or try to hide your mistakes. You are grounded about realising that mistakes happen, and courageous enough to admit them.

Perfectionism in Relationships – Green
You bring to your relationships a healthy degree of openness and frankness. Be sensitive to friends or partners who have less strength in this area. Remember that their behaviour is likely to stem from an overly critical inner voice.

EXPLORE:

- Notice and be proud that you can allow your mistakes to be visible, which creates space for learning and growth.

- It is worth thinking about how you got to this place. Growth in partnerships needs constant nurturing.
- Is your partner/friend as robust as you in this area? If not, have you explored why?

TIPS:

- Don't take this for granted, but enjoy this capacity.
- It may be easy to slip into a comfortable way of being together, and life might need to be spiced up sometimes.
- Look back and laugh together at your earlier disasters.

Perfectionism in the Family – Green

Your ability to admit your mistakes can be a good model for other family members. Others in the family may benefit from awareness and guidance in this area.

EXPLORE:

- Owning up to mistakes is a generous thing, but make sure it doesn't slide into a way of not being bothered about them.
- You may find it easy to own up to mistakes, others might not – you might need to understand that they find it harder than you.
- You are probably consistent with your rules and boundaries, irrespective of your mood.

TIPS:

- Treat mistakes as learning opportunities – without making mistakes, we cannot grow.
- As a family, reminisce together about disastrous holidays, trips, DIY works. Emphasise how catastrophic they felt at

the time, but how funny they seem in retrospect, and what you all learned.

- If you do slide into being more unpredictable than your usual self, don't let others give you a hard time for it.

Perfectionism in the Workplace – Green

You will make a trusted and trustworthy employee. You are unlikely to sweep mistakes under the carpet, and you will be able to defuse escalating situations early. Your lack of fear about making a mistake is reassuring to others as they are never 'left in the dark'.

EXPLORE:

- How do your colleagues or seniors respond when mistakes are owned up to?
- Do you make a point of trying not to repeat the same mistakes?
- Do you point out others' mistakes when they fail to?

TIPS:

- Encourage others to recognise that you can learn a great deal from mistakes if you take responsibility for them and analyse them.
- As a boss or colleague, recognise that for others in the team it may take significant courage for them to admit difficulties.
- Allowing others to reflect on their mistakes as opposed to whistleblowing is a difficult area to negotiate.

If you code blue for perfectionism

You exhibit a strong desire to want to look as good as possible. You have a subconscious tendency to hide your mistakes/cover your tracks, fearing you will be in trouble if you are found out. This characteristic is difficult to recognise, so you will really need to question yourself.

Perfectionism in Relationships – Blue

You may have difficulty in facing up to the consequences of your actions. Find people you trust to have your best interests at heart rather than their own and practise tolerating benign or constructive criticism from partners or friends. A conscious decision to share your vulnerabilities will be helpful, but it is an uncomfortable process and requires a degree of courage. However, it can help self-growth.

EXPLORE:

- Were you overly criticised as a child? Do you recall being scared?
- Do you hide your 'mistakes' from your partner/flatmates? An error in bookkeeping? An argument with your mother-in-law?
- Do you want to look perfect to your partner, and therefore cannot reveal your whole self?

TIPS:

- Learning to trust that others can have an appropriate reaction is a hard journey, but now is the time to start.

- Pause and think when partners or friends 'criticise' your errors. Are they really being critical? Or are they actually being supportive, trying to make light of the situation?
- Learning that you might be loved even if you are known to your very core is something you might need to work on, or need help with.

Perfectionism in the Family – Blue

There is a tendency for an overly criticised child to repeat the pattern with their own children, partners or younger family members. As you like to hide your mistakes, this is one brain domain where insight is particularly difficult.

EXPLORE:

- Do you respond angrily to small misdemeanours? Is your bark worse than your bite?
- Do you realise that you still tend to hide your own mistakes? From your children? Your siblings? Your parents?
- What do you fear from your family's responses to you?

TIPS:

- Avoid aggressive discipline. Remember that your size alone may be intimidating to a child and perhaps temper your response.
- Try to be honest with younger family members about your own mistakes. They will learn from your example.
- Even though you expect perfectionism from yourself, maybe realise that it is not reasonable to expect it from others.

Perfectionism in the Workplace – Blue

Your desire to avoid mistakes may result in you being a conscientious and cautious employee. Your meticulous attention to detail and your drive to do things perfectly will mark you out as someone to be relied on. Many successful finance directors have this characteristic. But, on the other hand, it is possible that your reluctance to acknowledge errors may be recognised, and may limit progress in your career.

People with blue in this domain often find their way into jobs where it is almost impossible to make a mistake, where the responsibility for decision-making is limited and the work is fact- and figure-based, and where the consequences of any necessary decision-making are laid at someone else's door. But if we never make mistakes, we do not grow.

EXPLORE:

- What do you do if you make a mistake? What do others in your work environment do?
- How do you feel about a colleague when they own up to a mistake? Do you recognise that this increases your trust in their integrity?
- Do you misinterpret support as criticism?

TIPS:

- Remind yourself regularly that being human means just that; balance a need for high quality with an awareness that we all make mistakes.
- Think long and hard about the potential consequences of your mistakes. Read the story of the spanner on the runway.
- Take a deep breath and admit your mistakes. You will learn to appreciate the sense of relief this brings.

Case Study: The Story of the 'Spanner on the Runway'

There is a true story of 'the spanner on the runway': a naval aircraft mechanic on an aircraft carrier realised that he had left a spanner on the runway. Knowing that it was likely to cause an accident, he immediately owned up to it, expecting to be demoted. The landing was aborted and a disaster was averted. Instead of suffering what he feared, however, he was praised for owning up so quickly to a mistake that could have had consequences.

Rebelliousness

Do people tell you that you are defiant, whether you agree with them or not? Have you ended up with something you don't really want just because it is something someone else didn't want you to have? Have you said no to something helpful because your response was a reflex?

Or are you able to make your own judgements on issues that affect you and take advice well, using a mixture of your own common sense and others' recommendations?

Consider a guest at a dinner party. If offered an open choice between a glass of red wine and a glass of white wine, she will opt to take the red. However, if the tray is offered to her with, 'I think you'll absolutely love this red,' her response becomes, 'No, thank you, I'll have a white.' Even though she is really keen to sample the red.

This sort of behaviour may seem somewhat perverse but the explanation lies in the person's rebelliousness domain marker.

Where does rebelliousness come from?

Between the ages of seven and ten years old, or the latency period, a young child generally has an innate trust of authority and is usually happy to go along with the rules. In fact, children this age often adhere to the rules more than the adults around them.

So, a parent says to a child, 'We're going to the museum today and not the park, because that's what I want to do.' The child may not like it, and may act out a bit, but in general it's a pretty straight-forward transaction and no one is pretending anything else. Consider, however, what happens when the parent presents the situation as: 'We're going to the museum today because you'll have more fun,' and then proceeds to sit in the museum café, having coffee with friends the whole afternoon. The dynamic of this trans-action is much more confusing for the child: the decision appears to have been good for the adult rather than for the child, even though the adult is saying otherwise. Of course, it's a question of degree and nobody needs to worry too much about prioritising the occasional cup of coffee. But, depending on when and how often a child receives these conflicting messages about motiv-ation, they can end up with a cynical mistrust of the authority behind them, because the intrinsic message is manipulative.

The key here is the element of manipulation and motivation – the adult convincing a child that a decision is all about them, when actually it is nothing to do with the child. Sometimes the adult will do this deliberately – they just want their own way but cannot bring themselves to acknowledge this because it makes them look bad – but more often than not it is totally unconscious. Some children then cannot help themselves and, as a subconscious statement about their awareness of the mixed messages, they go against the decision or request being made. Even if the best thing for the child is to say, 'Yes,' they still say, 'No.' A rebel is being created.

This domain is about the motivations and convolutions that can underlie apparently simple instructions. Sometimes there may be a conflict between two authorities: a mother offers to play a game of chess with her child, and the child is delighted. However, the father prefers to go for a walk, and that is what they end up doing. The mother passes this off to the child as, 'I knew you would really prefer the walk,' but the child realises that the decision was really all about appeasing the father and may feel betrayed. So, how will the child react? For some, it will be, 'Whatever you like . . . Do I like chess? Not a clue . . . But I'll go along with what you suggest. I'll appease too.' But for others, it will be, 'I'm not buying into this. I'm not going for a walk.'

Depending on the circumstances, a young child may find it quite disturbing when authority is insisted upon. In some situations, authority figures may be very domineering in their determination that instructions should be followed, and the child may end up feeling humiliated. In others, the child may have unspoken concerns that they are unwittingly contributing to conflict between two parental authorities (see the scenario below of the teenage party). When events of this sort accumulate, they disrupt the child's usual transition from typical childhood obedience to a healthy adult respect for authority.

POINTS TO CONSIDER:

- Do you recall occasions as a child when you outwardly agreed to something being done 'for you', while feeling internally resentful and angry because it was obviously for someone else?
- Be consistent with rules for youngsters. Unpredictability in your own approach to life is likely to lead them to be more unpredictable in their own response to authority. A contentious decision will be perceived as a poor decision.
- Drive, in adult life, comes from a healthy adolescent development, so don't be tempted to 'squash' teenagers too much. Try to work out what is about safety and what is your own need to win a battle.

Rebelliousness in everyday life

People with a less marked characteristic of rebelliousness have an easier relationship with authority. They acknowledge that authority does not automatically lead them to a sense of inferiority, and that authority can, if needed, be questioned in a straightforward and reasonable manner. The more marked rebels feel that submitting to authority is a humiliation. People with a strong characteristic of rebelliousness may have been made to feel inferior in the past, perhaps by parents who have been humiliated themselves.

This authority figure could be represented by a doctor, a teacher, a boss. It is someone in your subconscious world who appears to be asking something of you that makes you feel like a child and doesn't allow you agency or choice. As a result, you cannot help rebelling, even if by doing so you choose a less satisfactory option. You are quite happy to 'cut off your nose to spite your face'. And you may or may not have a considerable degree of insight into this tendency.

Sometimes this rebellious streak will take an individual down an exciting, novel route. A blue marker in this domain is common, for example, in many entrepreneurs and often co-exists with the blue entrepreneurial domain. However, there is a worry that rebellious people may end up on paths that don't particularly suit them, simply because they choose to take the opposite one to that suggested by an authority figure. On other occasions, although they ostensibly follow the directed pathway, they do things in such a way as to subconsciously sabotage the process in a more 'passively aggressive' way.

It is worth noting that rebellious behaviour doesn't always present itself in an obvious manner. It may be manifested much more subtly than by outright insubordination or disagreement. There is the example of a teacher who was unhappy in her job. Through exploring her coding in this area, she realised that her mother (who had also been a teacher) had been very keen for her to follow the same career. Although she did not get on particularly well with her mother, she did as instructed. She derived no enjoyment from the job, and was overly strict with the children, as indeed her mother had been with her. She was effectively passing her anger at her mother down the line. If a rebel cannot bring themselves to create conflict directly, they can take control by being seemingly agreeable in a passive-aggressive way that is difficult to define and also very hard to deal with.

In relationships, there is often one person who appears to be a rebel and one who likes to please, in an apparent attraction of opposites. This may represent a well-balanced partnership, but in psychological terms, these two people may both have an imbalance in their relationship with authority: an over-pleaser and an under-pleaser, if you like. There is an underlying instability to the dynamic, which can flip when the rebel eventually pushes the pleaser too hard: their resulting 'NO!' may be a loud one.

Case Study: The Teenage Party

Sara recalls a particular incident in her teenage years when she was seventeen and wanted to go to a party. Her rather strict mother thought this particular party was inappropriate, and refused to take her. Sara approached her father, who, wanting his peace on a Friday evening, agreed. A row between the parents ensued, and although Sara got what she wanted, there was a strained atmosphere at home for a few days.

Deep down, Sara knew her mother was probably right to have reservations about the party. Although she was angry about her mother's decision, if her father had been aligned with it, she would probably have accepted things (after a teenage sulk). Instead, she had unwittingly caused conflict between her parents, and subconsciously she believed that this was her fault.

Sara decided that if parenting decisions were always associated with this degree of conflict, it would be better to skip them altogether. In future, better to head off to parties without asking anyone.

It is important to remember that, as with all the domains, the rebelliousness domain does not exist in a vacuum. It interacts with all the other brain domains, and may only be activated in response to certain provocations. The rebel responds differently to different levels of opposition. Whereas the opposition of a small child might fail to activate someone's rebellious streak, someone in a peer group or in authority might provoke tension. This is why, ultimately, the true rebel may work most successfully either as their own boss or at the head of a hierarchy. Or, by learning to accept that a boss's decisions can, in fact, be trusted.

Case Study: The Silent Rebellion

Jude is asked by a friend: 'Can you come to Sunday lunch?' 'Love to,' he answers. 'What time?' '1 p.m. sharp.' 'OK,' says Jude. But then he turns up an hour late.

Jude's partner asks, 'What would you like to do today?' 'Anything you like,' replies Jude. 'Let's go to the beach and paddle with the children,' suggests Jude's partner. 'Don't forget your waterproofs, it's cold today.' 'Great,' says Jude. He arrives on time at the beach. But in his shirt-sleeves, without his waterproofs.

Jude's boss sends him an email scheduling a meeting in the Board Room for nine o'clock. 'Fine,' Jude pings back. At two minutes to nine, he takes an 'important' phone call that prevents him from attending the meeting.

This is a passive-aggressive way of living these things out, which is very hard to define and respond to. It is a passive kind of sabotage. The person hasn't been able to say, 'Well, actually, no, I don't want to come for lunch with you, I want to go out with my girlfriend.' They cannot bring themselves to create an immediate web of conflict, so they take back control by actions, not words, and communicate aggression in a way that is very hard to define.

If you code green for rebelliousness

You have no particular subconscious tendency towards oppositional thinking. You do not instinctively mistrust authority figures and hierarchy but you also trust your own judgement. You are comfortable being directed and don't mind being told what to do if it is appropriate – you are happy to learn from others. You use a mixture of your own common sense and others' recommendations to arrive at a decision which is yours.

Rebelliousness in Relationships – Green

You are happy in collaborative relationships; decisions are made between the couple. You are also happy if you or your partner need to make the decision due to time or expertise. You find it easy to trust another without being naive.

EXPLORE:

- You can hear your partner's advice but you make your own decision.
- Can you offer advice but not be offended when it is not taken up?
- Do you sometimes feel your relationships are too steady?

TIPS:

- Don't underestimate what a special quality this is.
- You probably don't take offence easily, but bear in mind that others may be more sensitive and you may have to communicate more carefully with them than they have to with you.
- Cut loose your inner rebel from time to time. You never know, you and your partner may enjoy it.

Rebelliousness in the Family – Green

With your more balanced tendency, you are well positioned to cope with the rebels in the family. You are likely to cope equally with the vagaries of grandparental interference and teenager rebellion, or challenging siblings. But, again, be aware of the mix of domain types surrounding you.

EXPLORE:

- You are not really rebellious, so can it be a shock when children are rebellious?
- Consistency is your gift – do you create this for others?
- Do you think your teenagers tend towards outward rebellion or inward resentment?

TIPS:

- Remind yourself that rebellious behaviour is a particular feature of teenage development and growth. Keep reminding yourself of this.
- Try communicating what it is that enables you to be consistent, rather than just being it. Your children can learn from the outward expression.
- Helping your teenagers to express their anger and their love towards you helps the long-term grievances.

Rebelliousness in the Workplace – Green

You make a good employee. Your response to authority is balanced: you engage appropriately and respond well to feedback. You can manage and in turn be managed without feeling compromised. Be aware, though, that there may be a tendency to allow the views of others to dominate in order to avoid conflict.

EXPLORE:

- You can take advice, arriving at your own decisions and assessing risks for yourself.
- Maybe you feel exasperated when another in your vicinity can't do that?
- Do others who seem either unable to stand up for themselves or have made a contrary decision bemuse you?

TIPS:

- You may be envious of those who get more attention from being rebellious.
- Be aware that you may be well suited to a career in an organisation with clear structure.
- You may flourish with a strong mentor with whom you can talk through managing feisty people.
- You may need to push yourself to make your voice heard. Speak out more.

If you code blue for rebelliousness

You have an inherent dislike of being told what to do. People have often told you that you are defiant. From time to time, you may find it useful to channel this tendency, but be aware that there is a risk that others find you ungovernable or intransigent. You may find yourself at odds with people who try to set limitations on your behaviour. On the positive side, however, you may be feisty, energised and fun.

Rebelliousness in Relationships – Blue

With this domain coding, you are likely to couple with someone who wants to please you, but be aware that if you push them too far and keep pushing too often, they may come out of their shell and explode.

EXPLORE:

- Do you insist on something your partner doesn't want you to have? And end up with something you don't really want?
- Do you have a reflex negative response to helpful suggestions?

Or,

- Do you passively aggressively say yes to things, but then do the opposite?

TIPS:

- Take a minute to make the decision about what you really want, rather than rebelling against your partner or friends' recommendation.
- Try to develop a capacity for stepping back and thinking rather than giving a knee-jerk 'no'.
- Remember that it can be wearing for others to exist in a constantly high-octane environment, or with unspoken but clear aggression.

Rebelliousness in the Family – Blue

The presence of a rebel or two can work wonders for the family in terms of energy levels, but an excess of rebellious coding can tip the family dynamic into situations of repeated conflict.

Rebellious parents can often be wonderful with a child when they are little, but when the child becomes a teenager and seeks their own authority, the parent has to rebel against the child, which is very difficult. The parent believes the child is rebelling against the parent, but look more closely – who is rebelling against whom?

EXPLORE:

- Think about when you were growing up – were you distrustful of authority and did you rebel when you were too young?
- Do you react badly to advice from relatives? Parents-in-law? Siblings?

Or,

- Do you rebel by adopting passive aggressive behaviour rather than outright disagreement?

TIPS:

- You may have learned not to trust authority, but now you are an adult, that is likely to be more of a hindrance than a help.
- Recognise that your own teenagers may feel the same. Work out if clashing with them is keeping them safe or if it's more about you rebelling against them.
- Be gracious when others want to help. Learn to accept the proffered hand rather than biting it.

Rebelliousness in the Workplace – Blue

A blue rebelliousness may bring energy and drive that can be a tremendous asset in the workplace. However, a little goes a long way. You may find it difficult to take instruction, and there is a risk that you are perceived as difficult to manage. Many people with this coding end up in a career where they have no peer group or boss.

EXPLORE:

- Are you aware that you dislike being directed? Does this lead you to places that you don't want to go?
- Are you making the most of your entrepreneurial instincts?
- Can you identify a mentor whose advice you actually would accept and trust?
- Can you be brave enough to acknowledge the impact of your behaviour on others?

TIPS:

- You may enjoy working for yourself. Think about really tapping into your inner rebel and driving your own venture – with your reluctance to take 'no' for an answer, you could go far.
- The nature of this domain is that you don't trust easily. Really try to find someone whom you trust who can challenge you on the way.

Authenticity

Do you need to know what is in the other person's mind before you can make a decision? Do you adamantly refuse to care about what is in another's mind?

Or do you swing through life, not concerning yourself with what others think of you?

Are you the person whose social-media photo is as perfect as it can be? Do you list your real interests on social media, or those which you think make you look good? Do you always apply make-up before leaving the house? Do you bite your tongue if you think your real opinion might reflect badly on you? Do you worry that a new relationship will feel good for a few months, but that when the other person gets to know you it will all go wrong?

This brain domain is all about controlling your self-image and the way other people perceive you. To do this, you have a fantasy that you can control another's mind, so they will only think what you want them to.

Where authenticity comes from

An interesting book was written by one of the great psychoanalysts, Wilfred Bion, in his old age, after his mother had died. He talks about the idea of 'false self', and how he had known since he was very young that his mother was so fragile that he had to cover up his true self and create a false self around it, so that she only saw what was good in him, because she could not cope with the bits that he felt were bad. It is this combination of fragility and control in a parent that creates a child's need to hide parts of their selves. They learn to hide those authentic parts deeper and deeper inside themselves, creating a front to the rest of the world. As they grow, they can't understand why it is so difficult to make contact with another; they believe they are so good, why don't other people get close to them? So then they become even more controlled, because they think maybe the other person is still seeing something bad in them, and this becomes a self-perpetuating disconnect.

Some people do this by always looking perfect, others do it by becoming obese or heavily tattooed or pierced. One of their subconscious aims is to become invisible by hiding behind a façade. These forms of control also change the skin that contains and holds us together, sometimes creatively but sometimes in a way that is harmful. This is a way of showing the world that our whole being feels 'unheld', in danger of bursting, and lets the world know without words that we feel unable to hold ourselves together.

There are many ways to become invisible. The best way, though it is often largely unconscious, is by trying to control what the other person sees. A parent's fragility may be obvious; for example, a physical fragility due to ill-health. But more often than not it is a mental fragility. The parent can appear ostensibly very controlling, but a child inherently realises that this apparent control is built on a fragile foundation. The parent may be able to cover this up to the outside world, and this is disturbing to a child: they see the fragility, they live with it, but the outside world does not recognise it. The family's authentic character, a mixture of good and bad, as in most families, gets hidden from the world behind a façade of perfection. The response of a child may sometimes be to act up, with extreme or erratic behaviour that makes the under-lying difficulties public to the outside world. Or, alternatively, they may learn to present a façade both to their parents and to the world, thereby shielding the turmoil from view. They become less and less 'authentic'.

This survival mechanism may work for whatever reason when someone is young, but as they grow up, it gets really difficult. If someone cannot be seen, how do they let another in far enough to have a relationship? How do they learn not to try to control the mind of the other? They are likely to form a relationship with someone who seemingly quite likes to be controlled, although that person will probably have their own ways of being controlling back. Controlling and appeasing are two sides of the same coin, but what they all aim for is to make sure that the person cannot be known. Being known is too dangerous for this person because they have an unconscious belief that this will upset someone else and that person won't respond in the way that is hoped, and rejection will follow.

A highly controlled person may develop sensitive 'antennae' that monitor the responses in other people, so that they can adjust their own behaviour accordingly. It may feel to them as though they are offering the other person an opportunity to have a say in the interaction. But the reality is that they are attempting to control the other person's perception of them. This constant monitoring is exhausting for the person trying to control things, and frustrating for the onlooker, who realises that they are only seeing part of a person and that they are not reaching the other person's authentic self. The end result is that, although they may be quite happy to be around the person, they may not fully incorp-orate them into their group.

A person's 'messy/unlovely' bits can be concealed in a variety of ways. Some mimic or mirror back what is in front of them, in order to appear like-minded and friendly. Others put on a dazzling display to draw the eye away from the true self – for example, with the use of flamboyant clothes, heavy piercing, prolific tattooing or cosmetic surgery. Or sometimes the concealment takes the form of only revealing the 'bad' side and concealing the normal, authentic good/bad mix. This is the child in school who looks and behaves as if they can't learn, despite the teacher knowing full well that they are bright. It may be that the child fears outperforming a sibling, or that the appearance of stupidity affords them protection from bullying. The effect is the same: to deflect the onlooker from perceiving their intelligence.

Case Study: Hiding His True Intelligence

A teacher in a school has in his class a belligerent boy who is assumed to have learning difficulties. One day the teacher asks the class a difficult maths question concerning how much money they would win in a football pool on a certain bet. The child's interest is sparked, he forgets himself and answers perfectly. The teacher's response is to look at the students, point two fingers at his own eyes and point the same fingers at the student – busted! The student's real self has been seen by the teacher, and the proper work can begin.

What starts as a survival mechanism in a child carries through into the relationships of adult life. Somewhere along the line they believe they have received the message that what they are, deep down, is not what others like. So they don't let others see them for who they really are. The majority of people, however, have learned through formative experiences that those close to them accept both their good and their bad characteristics. They grow up allowing others to see their true self. They are happy in their own skin. They are who they are, regardless of who might be around.

POINTS TO CONSIDER:

- In your childhood, was there a fragile adult who you felt the need to protect? Do you think that this may have had a long-term impact on the way you engage with others?
- Try to present your true self in front of children. Try not to collapse in front of them too often; equally, it is important to show them you can be vulnerable but recover, sad but come through it and laugh again. They will then feel less alone in their own emotional ups and downs. They won't tend to blame themselves.
- Allow children to show all their facets (weak, messy, gorgeous, helpful, unhelpful, ordinary) without over-reacting. Try to notice if you aren't coping with your children's emotions: i.e., do you hate them feeling sad? Try to manage your own self with honesty. Be open with your emotional responses so they feel they can express themselves without making you feel emotionally out of your depth.

Authenticity in everyday life

We all control our self-image to some extent, because of the innate human desire to be loved. But there is a spectrum: we may all suck our stomach in for the odd photograph, but we don't all feel the need to follow punishing diets to get rid of it. It is one thing to put our best photographs on social media, quite another to have social-media photos so out of sync with our real appearance that we avoid meeting anyone in person.

The green authentic person tends to be consistent in the side they present. Green authenticity goes hand-in-hand with clear boundaries: if someone tries to push them around, they know who they are and can respond clearly with, 'No, actually I'm not going to do that, it wouldn't be good for me.'

The blue authentic person presents themselves in an inconsistent manner, altering themselves to suit the person or group they are with. They are chameleons, adjusting their character to match their audience. As a result, they might find themselves uncomfortable at a wedding, or a similar big gathering where their different friendship groups from different walks of life are all present in the one room. As they are not confident in who they are at any given time, their boundaries tend to be less clear: they can allow themselves to be pushed into difficult situations where they are out of their comfort zone. Afterwards, their fingers burnt, they may end up making even greater efforts to control the way they are seen.

Continual subconscious manipulation of their image in this manner can be exhausting. Exhausting too for the person (colleague, friend, partner) on the receiving end: they are constantly trying to see through all this to the real person. The subconscious desire of the blue domain is to avoid detection of their supposedly less appealing characteristics, but their behaviour in fact renders it more difficult for anyone to get close to the real, likeable them. It requires time and patience to let people in far enough to have true relationships. We need to learn gradually that what we believe to be a shameful part of us is actually not as damaging as we think. Possibly it is actually totally normal, and even charming or endearing to those who love us.

If you code green for authenticity

You have a secure sense of self, which you communicate consistently. You are not driven subconsciously to control what you reveal of yourself or how others experience their time with you. You are comfortable in your own skin. Other people will tend to recognise that you message who you are, and will see you as genuine.

Authenticity in Relationships – Green

You are centred in your own belief and self-worth, and as a result you have the ability to be upfront with others. You are happy to 'let down your guard' early in friendships or when dating, either online or in real life. As a relationship progresses, you may require less energy than others to maintain it, as you do not have to work on controlling how the other person sees you. Being honest about who you are means that you are likely to be attracted to others whom you can read well.

EXPLORE:

- Do you feel secure in your skin?
- With a green authentic brain, because you do not have to control how others see you, it takes you less energy to swing through life.
- Do you ask others when you sense you are not getting the 'whole picture'?

TIPS:

- Be aware that not everyone is as open as you are. What you see is not necessarily what you get.
- Although being truly 'authentic' is a great thing, be wary of not wanting to sometimes dress up well for

another who loves you anyway, but needs to feel special sometimes.

- You tend to message who you are, and people feel you are genuine, but those who hide themselves might actually find you quite terrifying because you are not easily controlled.

Authenticity in the Family – Green

The green brain has not had to protect a fragile (or apparently fragile) parent or lover, so they can learn to grow and be who they are. They learn they can be angry and recover from anger; that the other person has survived their anger and has not lashed back or been destroyed by it.

Your confidence in yourself provides a bedrock for the security of the family. Be sensitive to others less robust about the image that they project.

EXPLORE:

- Can you identify others in the family who are less confident in expressing their true selves?
- How supportive of them are you?
- Are there any aspects of yourself that you keep hidden from your partner? Parents? Siblings?

TIPS:

- Provide the more vulnerable in the family with plentiful reassurance about their lovability.
- Don't unmask them in front of others.
- Don't forget in your authenticity that a little acting and drama can be fun with partners.

Authenticity in the Workplace – Green

Your ability to present your true self at work will inspire confidence in those around you and will help you forge ahead. Colleagues know that 'what they see is what they get'. There is no spin from you; they will be able to trust your clear reactions and accept your support through their own successes and failures.

EXPLORE:

- Does the ability to always be yourself help you in dealing with the vagaries of colleagues?
- Are you good at combining instinct and evidence when hiring?
- Do colleagues rely on you?

TIPS:

- Your internal scaffolding is very secure – don't forget you will be fine in a variety of environments.
- You probably hire very steady people, just be aware that some tasks might need more flair, but this might come with management issues that upset you. An authentic self is far more likely to manage diversity well.
- You may well like being relied upon, but occasionally you feel resentful. Don't forget to let people know that your steadiness is not something to be taken for granted.

If you code blue for authenticity

You have a tendency to hide the 'real you', a subconscious desire to control what other people see of you. This does not mean that you are deliberately manipulative, but that you want to regulate and maintain the image you project. This can serve you well in some situations – strong mental containment and distance can be helpful. However, if you are constantly checking, editing and presenting yourself rather than just 'being' yourself, it can be mentally taxing and draining.

Authenticity in Relationships – Blue

When we begin relationships and friendships, either online or in person, most of us take a bit of time before we can be confident enough to reveal our authentic selves. A blue state of mind in the authentic domain, however, will take considerably longer than most. As your relationships progress and become more established, your partners and friends may develop a sense that you are not being authentic with them at all times, especially as you become more intimate. It may be tiring for those around you to keep trying to work out who you really are.

A person with this characteristic will need to develop the confidence and trust to begin to show who they really are. They need to understand that, even with all their imperfections, they truly are likeable. After all, if we actually were perfect, we would be very difficult to like because everyone else would feel so inadequate!

EXPLORE:

- How well do you think your partner and friends know the real you?
- Do you think your partner keeps areas of themselves hidden? Which?
- Do your friends have imperfections and flaws that you find endearing?

TIPS:

- Work on developing the confidence and trust to begin to know who you really are, and therefore show it.
- Rather than push those around you to be vulnerable, work out how you can be vulnerable first.
- Recognise that to your partner or friends your imperfections and vulnerabilities may be your most appealing aspects, even though you don't feel this.

Authenticity in the Family – Blue

Through proximity and history, your close family are those most likely to know the real you. This may help you or may worry you, depending on your experiences. Your blue domain may express itself more when you are worried about rejection.

EXPLORE:

- Do you feel you need to hide behind a 'front' for your family? Which members? In-laws? Stepchildren?
- Which particular aspects of yourself do you try to hide?

Or,

- Do you sometimes become more arrogant than you mean to be, and brag about aspects of your life which aren't as good as you make out?

TIPS:

- If you need to know what is in the other person's mind before you can make a decision yourself, you are struggling with showing your true self. Try asking yourself what you want and need. If this cripples you with shame, you might need some help to get out of it. If it just makes you feel anxious, try once a day to make a decision before you know what the other person wants.

- Try not to hide behind charm, weight, perfect make-up, the dark, your intellect, professionalism, your role, even though you might fear the consequences of being visible.
- You think it is safer to make yourself look better than you are, but people often know the truth anyway, and it might be worthwhile getting some help to think this through.

Authenticity in the Workplace – Blue

If you could worry less about how you project yourself, you would allow more of your genuine potential to flourish and be seen. You would have more energy; maintaining barriers is exhausting. On the plus side, being aware of the way you present yourself in the workplace can be a very positive attribute.

Case Study: Authenticity and Online Dating

An extract from *Grazia* magazine:

'Looking for love? Honesty really is the best policy'

How refreshing to see new data released by a dating app that shows that users who are honest about themselves get more matches. The app created badges so that daters can admit upfront that they live at home with parents or that they drink heavily – both possible red flags – and found that those who used them were more popular than those who kept info to a minimum. Turns out we don't want to find the 'perfect' person online – we just want to meet someone real.

EXPLORE:

- Do you keep your guard up to prevent colleagues from seeing the real you?
- Are you frustrated by a disconnect with your teammates? Or do you find it useful?
- Do you find work relationships and interfaces more draining than they should be?

TIPS:

- You may well fear rejection if people get close. Try to believe that people want to connect with you.
- At times you may feel very inwardly alone at work. There is no shame in seeking mentoring to find out why others find it difficult to get close to you.
- Being constantly on guard is exhausting – try letting go more, drop your guard, stride forward at work with more energy.

Neediness

Are you looking for emotional sustenance? Do you always want more approval, someone to tell you that you look ok, your work is good, your children are happy, because you can't quite tell yourself? Conversely, do you never ask for help?

Or can you ask for a reasonable amount of care from someone else, without driving them round the bend?

Consider how likely you would be to employ the person who writes the following on their CV:

- I am unable to make a decision for myself without first gaining approval from my boss or colleagues.
- I will need affirmation at each step of the task.
- Once the task is completed, I will require to be thanked and complimented.

But what if they also added:

- I will be unfailingly supportive and unstintingly nurturing of all the junior members of the department.

This person typifies the two facets of the blue domain for neediness: a very real requirement for support from others, combined with an enhanced capacity for providing nurture to others.

Where neediness comes from

Neediness is a dependent state of mind. It's a slide back to that unconscious age where we have not yet developed the internal scaffolding that enables us to soothe ourselves appropriately. We slip back to needing another person to assess our emotional well-being for us. This is quite a young age; the crucial period of development for this domain is from birth to two years, the period when a child is totally dependent on another person for their essential wellbeing. Initially, the carer has to interpret a baby's needs telepathically, without any verbal communication. The child can't say, 'I'm hungry.' They cry and the parent interprets the cues and provides food. They scream and the parent rocks them and reassures: 'You're ok, this tummy ache will pass. You're in pain.'

For a baby, needs are relatively simple: food, warmth, parental presence. As a child grows, however, their needs become increasingly complex and diverse and they learn to take on more responsibility for communicating this. At a relatively early age, they begin to demonstrate a requirement for adult approval. Creative play and drawing play important roles. In the early stages, the interaction tends to be along the lines of a parent observing: 'That's a beautiful tractor you've drawn,' and the child saying: 'No, it's a giraffe.' What the child needs is someone to see and approve of what they have drawn, even though it may be uninterpretable. As the child grows and develops, it becomes their responsibility to communicate to another (parent, teacher, sibling) what they have drawn – what their day has been like. They learn to have their own assessment of the world and to tell another what state of mind they are in.

Neediness is caught up in the stage of development where the child wants their parents to be telepathic. They don't want to have to say, 'I'm hungry'; they want the parent simply to know, for the food to be there the moment their hunger kicks in. They don't want to wait, or have a gap between expression and satisfaction. This state of mind is just beyond screaming but before we are able to put words to what we need. The parent has to guess. While a child is developing the verbal skills to express their needs more clearly, they also begin to realise that these needs are not always met with instant gratification. Increasingly, there arises a time lag between demand and supply. Work or household chores can intervene. 'I'm sorry, I have to finish this report and then I can play with you.' 'I have to fix the car and then I can take you to the park.' Interestingly, the person with blue in this domain is predisposed to stop themselves getting what they need. The child may attempt to circumvent the delay, until they learn that this approach tends to backfire: the child hides the car key, but the parent then spends so long looking for it that the expedition to the park has to be abandoned.

It is perfectly normal for this state of mind never to quite stop, but the green state is where most of it is outgrown. The adult realises not only that they have to communicate this need to another, but that those needs might be rejected, either because too much is being asked or because the other is willing but not able to satisfy that need.

As we grow up through all the stages of development, we gain words but we never quite lose that instinct to show rather than tell. How often have we said to our children, 'Use your words,' because they default to showing someone what they are feeling rather than explaining?

If we are emotionally deprived, we often lack a certain vocabulary as it is extremely difficult for us to name the feelings. The fewer words we can find to use, the more preverbal we become.

The younger our unconscious age, the more likely we are to slip down the developmental ladder. However, if we are emotionally well, we can find the words to describe our emotional states. The more connected our emotional language is, the more likely it is that we are able to get back up on the developmental ladder when something has caused us to slip off. To keep well, it is better to have ten words that match our inner state of mind than to have a thousand words that are disconnected from our real self.

This doesn't work when the parents, for whatever reason, are unable to fully parent. The children then have to take on the mantle of responsibility for themselves. However, these children have age-inappropriate responsibility, which can leave them later feeling either abandoned or neglected, and they often place these feelings into a younger sibling and nurture them well with empathy. Therefore, like many of us, they avoid their own pain. Or it might leave them very self-sufficient. They bury their own needs deep – but these are likely to pop up later in life.

Underlying all this is a belief that your parent is an extended part of you, who must telepathically know what to say to you and when. And it doesn't matter what the parent says; unless they find the exact word that is in the child's head, the parent will be a disappointment to them. They have not responded to their neediness. But because the child cannot tell the parent that word, because it is stuck in a pre-verbal world, their feelings become very difficult and they need even more. They feel the parent doesn't understand them.

Being over-available to a child can also work in the same way, because the child will copy the parent. If the parent believes they have a right to some time to themselves, the child will too, but if the parent over-nurtures, the child will not learn to give themselves satisfactory space. Although it may cause a parent the odd tearful moment, we generally accept that it is healthy for the child to eventually learn to say to them, 'Off you go, I'm playing with my friends now. What, you again? I'm really ok playing Lego with my friends.'

Children learn and develop by copying the example of the adults around them. They observe how adults nurture and meet their needs, and so they learn to do likewise: for example, the child who lines up all their teddies to feed them at a tea party, or the child who gently puts their doll to bed with a lullaby, or parks their tractor next to their bed. In time, they begin to practise these nurturing characteristics, perhaps a little over-exuberantly, on younger siblings or pets. The development of this domain intricately entwines the ability to bestow nurturing and reassurance on others with one's own need for nurture and reassurance. We find that underdevelopment of the one characteristic goes hand in hand with strength in the other. Neediness and nurture can go hand in hand; a sense of one's own unmet needs can lead to enormous empathy for and nurture of others who feel the same.

POINTS TO CONSIDER:

- Did you feel a bit smothered or over-protected growing up? Was it just you, or your siblings too? Do you think this has affected you?
- If you have children, remember that it is normal for levels of attentiveness towards them to fluctuate with their age, their birth order and your daily timetable. Problems only arise when there are extremes of attentiveness, or sudden inexplicable changes in the pattern that don't allow the family to talk about it.
- Respond to the child who requires extra nurturing, but guard against constant over-attention at the expense of

other children. Perhaps most importantly, voice for them that they might ordinarily feel jealous and want some time. Allow them their feelings.

Neediness in everyday life

As we have seen, for a child, there is an underlying belief that a parent will understand what they need and will respond accordingly. It's part of the early belief that your parent is an extended part of you, who must telepathically know what to say to you and when. Someone who comes out blue for neediness carries this belief into adult life, expecting others to understand their high levels of requirement and to provide stroking and reassurance. But although this is what they hope for and believe is normal, unfortunately this is simply not the case. We live in a world where people expect you to self-manage for the majority of the time, and to only ask for help when you are running into serious trouble.

The neediness domain, more than many of the domains, is associated with a degree of insight and self-assessment, which varies from day to day, fluctuating, for example, with levels of tiredness or stress. With green for this, we can usually look at our work and think, 'Yes, that's good enough today', or, 'That wasn't the greatest; I'll need to work on it tomorrow.' But on a difficult day, we might choose to seek reassurance from our colleagues or boss. In family life, again the green brain will generally just crack on, not worrying too much about parenting skills. But on a more fraught day, we check in with our friends. ('Oh my God, was that rubbish parenting? I just sent my child to school knowing they weren't feeling well.') We ask for help when we feel ourselves in a disaster zone, or when we are genuinely unsure whether we have made a good decision. And we can cope with the answer. ('That wasn't your best moment!') We have insight and a bit of ordinary neediness where we are able to think, 'I'm more anxious than usual this morning, I think I might need to touch base with a friend.'

Needy blues, on the other hand, always require approval. 'What do you reckon? Is it good?' This is not a request for constructive criticism. It is a request for stroking. Some friends may be willing to provide a lot of stroking, but when the demand is excessively draining in terms of time and emotional energy, the needy person may find that friends make themselves less available. That neediness gets greater when there is anxiety in the system, too. Then we may need that friend or older family member to say, 'Yes, I've been in that situation too, it will be alright,' or, 'That is a disaster; drop everything and go and pick up your sick child from school.' Most of us have a bit of ordinary neediness. It is, as with all the domains, a question of degree. Remember that part of over-neediness and under-neediness is a sense of having felt, at some critical point, very alone.

Consider the workplace environment. A manager hurries into the office, announcing, 'Don't forget the conference tomorrow. The paperwork is due at 9 a.m.' The team have been working on it all day. The green brain responds, 'Ok, on it. See you with the paperwork at 9 a.m.' and then thinks nothing more of it. The blue brain is perturbed. Why has the manager not said, 'The paperwork is due at 9 a.m. and I'm sure you've done an amazing job, thank you'? Even though the manager may have said this for six days out of seven, on this particular seventh day, the blue-brain employee will feel they have not been appropriately looked after. They are unable to see that the manager is generally a good boss, who happens to be busy and who expects the employee to be able to look after themselves on this particular occasion.

Of course, there are managers who are not nurturing at all, and people who are needy don't cope very well with them – in fact, some needy people will hook themselves to this kind of boss just to prove that those in a type of parental authority role are rubbish, bosses are rubbish. It is like a public display of the lack you feel: you want everyone else to know that you have been (and are still being) parentally neglected.

In the home environment, many will identify with the tendency for a couple to descend into a neediness competition at the end of a long day:

A: 'You came home from work and you didn't see that I'd had a really hard day. But you must have known, because I'm still in my pyjamas and the dishes aren't done. How could you not have immediately understood that I needed your support?'

B: 'I'm very sorry, I was too tired to notice that you were still in your pyjamas and that the breakfast was still on the table. But from now on, I'll try to be more observant.'

A: 'I can't understand how you didn't know.'

B: 'Sorry, but I've actually had a terrible day at work and my boss had a real go at me. So why didn't you realise that? I'm home late, anxious and exhausted.'

A: 'Well, how am I meant to know that? I'm not psychic. You're often home late.'

B: 'Well, that's because I've often had a bad day! I have a difficult job.'

Temporarily, the couple are both needy children, and it is very difficult for them to reach out and look after each other. Green self-nurturers will, for the most part, be able to negotiate their way out of the situation. ('Alright, let's have tea and I'll tell you about my bad day and you can tell me about yours.') For the green brain, the skill lies in being able to judge one's own level of emotional stability on any one particular day. 'It's not been a great day, but, you know what, actually I'm ok, I can deal with it,' or, 'It's really not great today; I need to communicate this and find help.' With the blue brain, however, there is no insight. The situation easily spirals downwards. Or the couple may achieve a fragile containment that both parties know can break very easily, in which case neither feels very safe and happy. They resemble two young children trying to reassure each other: 'Don't worry, someone will be here soon.' (Pat pat.) 'Don't cry, they're on their way.' (Pat pat.)

A similar version of this dynamic can develop between a parent who has blue neediness and their teenager. The parent has been working away and comes home tired, to find the teenager sitting (phone attached) at the kitchen table. The parent says, 'I really like it when you have supper with me.' The teenager says, 'Yes, it is nice. Can I go out now?' The parent is feeling needy, unable to self-nurture, and wants the child to fill the hole. They expect the child to understand telepathically that they would like them to stick around. They forget that teenagers need at times not to have to empathise, but to move on with their lives.

If you code green for neediness

You do not need to seek a great deal of approval from others in order to experience a sense of self-worth. Although you may appreciate reassurance, you are balanced about the level of input you require. For the most part, you can maintain a sense of well-being without too much affirmation. You recognise that some days are more stressful than others, and you aren't afraid to seek advice and support appropriately to help you through these times.

Neediness in Relationships – Green

Although you are generally balanced in your requirement for stroking, your need might increase in times of stress and this must be communicated to those close to you. Bear in mind that seemingly external opposites tend to attract with this code. This probably won't be between green and blue in this domain, but is more likely to be between a blue over-needy person and a blue under-needy one. In this situation, there is outward difference but similar experiences that have led to the way the mind manages desire, the need for attention and the offering of nurturing to others. You may well find that if you desire attention you are attracted to someone who can always be there for you, but it's worth remembering that this fills the other's own neediness without it having to be openly expressed. They nurture to receive attention.

An extremely self-sufficient person does not rely on anyone else, and so has no need for anyone. They don't tend to enter into relationships where they are dependent on another, so they may stay on their own in life. But some neediness is really important. All of us should be able to feel that another person is potentially of value and can offer us something. A person who can rub along with others, interact, compromise, has to lose some of their independence.

EXPLORE:

- Is your need for attention generally met to your satisfaction?
- Do you feel that you value your partner and yourself in equal measure?
- Are you offering enough adventure in your relationship?

TIPS:

- You can generally give and receive attention in equal measure. Revel in this.
- You probably don't have to measure the give and take too closely with someone who is like you, but pay more attention in relationships where there is more difference.
- Watch out that intimacy does not become stale – one can get comfortable very quickly.

Neediness in the Family – Green

You don't require excessive affirmation from those around you, but you will need someone to reassure you when the going gets tough. You have a healthy attitude to allowing your children to grow and move away from you. You respond to their needs without smothering them. Teenagers exist in the no-man's-land between desperately needing their parents and desperately wanting them out of the way so that they can dispense with need altogether. They rollercoaster from one extreme to another. They slam the door in the parent's face and then sit on the other side of the door, desperately hoping for a hug. The job of the parent is to handle the rejection without rejecting the child back, to respond to the need even when it is not clearly articulated.

EXPLORE:

- Who do you turn to when you need affirmation. Parents? Siblings?
- Do you have a child who needs constant affirmation? Do you yet understand why?
- Do you get irritated when a family member repeatedly demands your attention?

TIPS:

- You may well be seen as generally ok – you may need to communicate to others (parents, siblings, friends) when you are feeling more in need of support than usual.
- It is usually good to respond to children who need some attention – there is generally a reason for it.
- You might be the sandwich generation, with elderly parents and young children. How does it feel? You are good at balancing everything, but some space for yourself won't go amiss.

Neediness in the Workplace – Green

You cooperate well with line managers. You are able to add to the output of the organisation without draining the team dynamics with requests for reassurance. You are comfortable working individually or where there is limited access to ongoing positive feedback.

EXPLORE:

- What circumstances push you to request reassurance?
- Are you patient enough with members of your team who need your repeated encouragement?
- Do you remember to give praise to those who nurture others in the team?

TIPS:

- You will thrive in positions of responsibility.
- Be aware that others require more reassurance than you. Be patient in providing it.
- Make sure you look for the nurturers – their supportive strengths are invaluable in a team.

If you code blue for neediness

You need a great deal of approval from others in order to experience a sense of self-worth. But your excessive desire to be nurtured goes hand-in-hand with an enormous capacity for nurturing and supporting others. You may well be aware of these tendencies in yourself.

Neediness in Relationships – Blue

When a person has too much neediness, it is like being in a constant baby state. When a baby is little, it needs the availability of the mother all the time. That is fine then, but when you are an adult, that wish for someone else's total availability becomes quite a burden for the other person. They are your colleague, or your boss or your partner, but not your mother. To play mother for someone the whole time can be wearing.

Within a relationship, someone who does not feel sufficiently 'stroked' can become envious, anxious or angry. They may need constant proof that they are indeed loved and will not be abandoned or rejected, and this often leads to intense and sometimes dependent relationships.

Mutual 'clinginess' may be normal and charming in the early stages of a new relationship: the headiness of romantic love which declares, 'I can't get enough of him/her.' But as the relationship progresses, excessive neediness may become overwhelming or exhausting for the other person.

You can be a delightful life partner or friend for someone as long as you have sufficient support from them and from others. You will find it easy to be supportive of your partner and friends, but you need the same level of support yourself. Alternatively, it is possible that you are so afraid of being over-needy that you squash any thought you have of wanting attention, leaving yourself looking over-self-sufficient. However, this may leave you not daring to connect with others who can offer you some, but not total, attention. This can be lonely.

EXPLORE:

- Are you overly anxious about your partner's wellbeing?
- Are you 'twitchy' if you are not contacted when you expect to be?
- We all love a friend who is telepathically in synch with us, but a real sign to watch out for is when we expect everyone to telepathically know our needs.

TIPS:

- You may have a tendency to overwhelm a potential partner or friend in the early stages of a new relationship. Watch this if you want it to go the distance.
- As the relationship progresses and deepens, learn to communicate that you require reassurance, rather than descending into envy, anxiety or anger.
- Notice when you stop communicating your needs with straightforward clarity, leaving another having to be telepathic to get it. You think you have expressed your needs and they are not responding: 'Do I have to spell out to you what's wrong? Can't you guess?' No, they really can't.

Neediness in the Family – Blue

You are the consummate nurturer, the parent looking after their brood. But who is looking after you? You will need regular affirmation and endorsement from your family about how good a job you are doing, whether that is as parent, child, sibling or as part of your extended family.

EXPLORE:

- How upset would you be if your birthday card failed to materialise?
- Do you often feel like your good deeds go unnoticed?
- Does your nurturing ever overwhelm?

TIPS:

- Constant nurturing is tiring. Your children will learn a valuable lesson about looking after their wellbeing by seeing you take some me-time to look after yourself.
- Learn to provide self-affirmation. Learn to give yourself positive feedback for family successes and achievements.
- Try not to let your children become outlets for your own high levels of neediness. Identify other ways to meet those needs – perhaps a chat on the phone with someone close? Notice when this is happening.

Neediness in the Workplace – Blue
You thrive on constant reassurance and validation. You respond to positive feedback, but you may find criticism hard to take. You will nurture the others in the team.

However, try to ensure that you are not the employee unable to make a decision for themselves without first gaining approval from the boss or colleagues at every step of the process. And once the job is completed, be aware of how much affirmation you need that it was a job well done.

Wanting approval, or 'stroking', at a very high level gives out a message that you can't be independent. When that happens in the workplace, the person is sending a message that they need their boss to be constantly available. What they often get back from their colleague or boss is that they aren't up to promotion because they can't be left alone to deal with things. They are not allowed to grow and prove themselves, to hold more responsibility.

EXPLORE:

- Could you stride forward more strongly if you were not constantly looking over your shoulder for affirmation?
- Do you feel anxious when your boss/colleagues do not praise you enough?
- Are you comfortable without regular one-to-ones with your boss?
- You may prefer to work in environments where lines of communication and feedback are regular and defined rather than sporadic.

TIPS:

- Train yourself to trust your own instincts about when you have done a good job.
- Try making your own assessment before you ask someone else. If that panics you, remember that you are equal to those who have gone before and you have the capacity to judge your own work, your own self.
- Conversely, do you determinedly never need help? Try sitting in the passenger seat sometimes. Remember, it is a part of the beauty of life to feel desire and need; don't underestimate your own capacity to remain stable if you need help – you will not end up powerless.

Graciousness

*Do you constantly need to make the other person feel
smaller, for fear of being overwhelmed? Do you get a kick
out of feeling bigger or more powerful than another? Do you
always set yourself up to be walked over?*

*Or do you have a good sense of your own existence and the
capacity to empathise without being overwhelmed?*

Try to picture yourself in the following situation: you have a workforce of twenty employees. Financial constraints require that one
of them is made redundant. There is one worker who has been
consistently less productive than the others. You hear on the
grapevine that this worker's family is suffering financial hardship.
Nevertheless, it is this employee that you select for redundancy.
The question is, how well do you sleep at night?

Where graciousness comes from

This domain focuses on our ability to identify and/or empathise
with others around us. In general, a person with a balanced gracious brain will have sufficiently robust boundaries that they can
make tough decisions about others, but with insight into the
effects these will have.

Graciousness relates to one of the earliest parts of our developmental pathway: the process of separation from our mother. After

nine months of maternal nourishment *in utero*, the umbilical cord is cut and a baby can survive as an independent entity. For the first few months, the mother's gaze is focused almost entirely on the baby, but gradually her gaze returns to other aspects of her life. The baby still cries at night for her attention, fighting the separation, but gradually realises that the mother has other things going on in her world. Mother and baby become a pair, rather than a single entity.

Our parental instinct prompts us to try to make that initial birth and separation from the womb as free from trauma as possible. We swaddle our baby to recreate a womb-like, coddled sensation, we cuddle and rock them to sleep. We hope that our children grow up with a healthy sense of themselves as a separate entity, confident in themselves and their own self. But sometimes the gradual nature of the separation is disrupted. For example, by a very abrupt weaning due to maternal illness. Or by the arrival of a new sibling very quickly, which results in the first child feeling they've been pushed aside at a very young age.

The way in which maternal separation is handled varies and individuals will have differing degrees of security in their own identity. We all have varying ability to identify/empathise with others around us. In general, someone with a balanced gracious domain will have sufficiently robust boundaries that they can make tough decisions about others, but with insight into their effects. The degree of thought involved in this decision-making is recognised by others, to whom they appear empathetic and 'gracious'. On occasion, we have an innate weakness around the concept of separation that may kick in, and we may over-identify. This means that we feel so like that person that we don't notice they are in fact different and cope differently. Then, if we are tasked with making a particularly tough decision, we are unable to disassociate ourselves fully from our effect on the other. At the extreme, we may descend into sleepless nights, agonising over our actions.

At the other end of the spectrum, particularly when the process of parental separation has been unduly traumatic and abrupt, our fear of total separation is so overwhelming that it is subconsciously suppressed. For these individuals, there is limited desire or ability to empathise with others. When difficult decisions are needed, these people are able to ride roughshod over others with equanimity and they perhaps even enjoy the power.

POINTS TO CONSIDER:

- Take stock of how often you transfer your own feelings to those around you – 'Put your jumper on.' (Because I'm cold.) 'You need something to eat.' (Because I'm hungry.)
- Help a child to become more gradually independent by supporting their decisions when they are safe and helping them to deal with the consequences. E.g. in cold weather, allow a child to say, 'No, thank you, I don't need my coat, I'm not cold.' Resolve to step forward with the coat only when they ask for it.
- You may want to consider the same approach to allow younger colleagues to mature in their role. Allow them to make their own decisions, but be prepared to step in to help them out when they struggle with the choice they made.

Graciousness in everyday life

In life and work, our 'graciousness' is apparent in the degree of thought we give to other people. Many of us lose sleep over tough issues concerning relationships at home and at work. The degree to which we are affected by this varies. Some people are sufficiently robust that they are only mildly aware; others become seriously anxious and stressed. The fundamental issue is, how securely do we live with the consequences of our decisions and their effect on others? How much support do we need from others to do so?

In the corporate sphere, the classic question is, as above, can you make someone redundant? If the answer to the question is yes, then you have good boundaries and can see that it is an essential part of keeping the 'body' of the corporation alive. You can go ahead and do it without too many emotional repercussions or feelings of guilt. One of the reasons why many CEOs have a limitation on their potential in this domain is that really good CEOs do mind if they have to attack their workforce in this way, and often feel that in some way it is a personal failure. In fact, they mind very much. This domain is sometimes called the 'gracious' brain because, although the CEO can do it, they have an empathetic understanding that, 'There but for the grace of God go I.'

If you are balanced in this domain, you are able to place yourself in the other man's shoes, but nevertheless you maintain a healthy degree of separation. The same concept applies in the broader spheres of life. In relationship terms, if you have to make a difficult decision about someone, can you make it with a degree of sympathy and empathy, but without over-identifying? Consider the young couple who were friends throughout university. They got it together at the end of their final year, in time for a wonderful, heady summer of love, foreign travel, parties and festivals. They started jobs in the same city, and shared interests, experiences and a common group of friends. But, for one of them, there was a gradual realisation that this was not enough, that they loved the other as a friend, but they were no longer romantically in love. How easily do they make the decision to break up the relationship? This person may know with absolute certainty that breaking up is the right decision, but if they are empathetic with the other (after all, it is their long-standing friend), they themselves may feel the hurt. They procrastinate. They solicit advice. They agonise with friends. The strain may take its toll. It takes significant robustness for one to be able to separate successfully from the other.

In the family setting, green in this domain brings to the table the valuable qualities of sympathy and sensitivity. But these people may recognise in themselves a tendency to over-identify with their children, agonising over the mini-traumas that are part and parcel of a child's daily existence. They feel the pain of being excluded in the playground, of being offered the part of Nana in the school play rather than Peter Pan, of losing the race on sports day. They generate feelings of anxiety in the child, who may actually have been happily engrossed in their book in the playground, or delighted to be the one allowed to wear the dog costume in the pantomime. Or perhaps they are disappointed but need help to manage this rather than join the emotional sense of disaster the parent has become hooked into.

At the other extreme, blue in this domain lacks the ability to sympathise and empathise. They sleep well at night, secure in their decision-making. Such robustness may be perceived as a valued asset in the workplace, but there is a fine balance, which can tip into insensitivity or even ruthlessness.

If you code green for graciousness

You are able to balance the existence and rights of yourself with the existence and rights of others. You can make difficult decisions affecting those around you, but you can empathise with their impact. You are generally able to self-regulate and control your own feelings of disappointment and distress. However, sometimes making tough decisions about family, friends or colleagues takes its toll on you. During these times you may need to be able to lean on others for support.

Graciousness in Relationships – Green

Your graciousness is balanced by the care, sympathy and empathy that you bring to your relationships.

With green in this domain, relationships are balanced and boundaried. There is an appropriate level of sympathy when there is a problem, with each partner knowing their own feelings. However, these people can often ignore someone without difficulty if, in their view, their problem is bigger than the other person's at that moment. They do not get caught up in someone else's difficulties. This can on occasion come across as cold and unsympathetic to other people.

EXPLORE:

- Does your empathy towards your partner and friends allow you to be supportive?
- You probably don't over-agonise about relationships, but can this appear dispassionate?
- Do you feel you have good boundaries? They are usually very helpful in a partnership.

TIPS:

- You probably know you have a right to exist as a separate individual within a couple – this will help when the going gets tough.
- Seeing things from each other's point of view is something you need to hold on to, but don't be overwhelmed or paralysed by it.

- Good boundaries are the key to good partnerships, but sometimes you might have to knowingly step over them to help another.

Graciousness in the Family – Green

In the family, you tend to be the glue and the balance that keeps things on an even keel. You have enough robustness to say no when no is the best answer for the growth and development of the individuals and the family, not because you enjoy being punitive. Yet you can also be empathetic to others' needs and understand what they might want from you and from others, even if you aren't able or don't want to give in.

EXPLORE:

- Do you feel at home in a family group, and a balanced parent?
- Are you balanced in your reactions to family traumas?
- Are you able to share your anxieties with friends and family, being honest with them when you are struggling?

TIPS:

- It is a great thing to belong easily. Remember this when the family disperses to other communities.
- What seems catastrophic to a child one day might be forgotten by the next. Stay with your instinct and find the appropriate response.
- When there are difficult family decisions to be made, sharing the burden of responsibility with your siblings or other relatives is probably helpful to you.

Graciousness in the Workplace – Green

You are sufficiently mentally robust to make tough decisions that involve others, but afterwards they may weigh heavily on you. You have an empathy and sensitivity that allows you to offer comfort and support to others. You have the potential to thrive and win respect in roles that involve leadership and responsibility. Others will be able to feel that you do not take tough decisions lightly and that you are sensitive to their pain: you are perceived as 'gracious'.

EXPLORE:

- Do you perceive it as a strength or a weakness that you feel the weight of people's issues?
- Does your empathy towards other people mean that you are highly regarded?

TIPS:

- Your very balanced centre means that you get asked to make tough people decisions.
- A good sense of your own existence and the capacity to empathise with colleagues is helpful, but watch out for being overwhelmed. Be mindful that roles that hold significant responsibility for others may cause you to be stretched.
- You are good at ceding your place to the person who needs it more than you at the moment, but keep a healthy sense of knowing when to step up for yourself.
- People can't bend you to their will, but sometimes that feels like being sidelined as some exciting people might walk away from you because you are not entering their personal drama. Don't be too envious of them – you have something that is really good.

If you code blue for graciousness

You may sometimes come across as a bit arrogant, which is a cover for your lack of self-identity. When it comes to making decisions affecting others, you are not predisposed to consider, or even sometimes to notice, the consequences of your actions. Blue coding is usually deeply ingrained and it is associated with limited insight: if you ask your friends to comment on something, you may often perceive their responses as criticism or threat. You will want people to agree with you.

Graciousness in Relationships – Blue

Be aware that you do not easily empathise with partners and friends. This may work well with other people who have blue here: you may be able to exist equably as 'islands in a stream'. But you may need to remind yourself that with green-domain partners and friends, empathy is usually an essential requirement for an ongoing and fulfilling relationship.

You may find yourself needing to constantly give way, or, conversely, impose your own wishes at all costs. Try taking the time to think about that reaction, and allow yourself to change your mind now and then – so, 'I was a bit hasty there; now I think about it, it might be nice to/I'd quite like to . . .' If you are someone who always gives way, dare to make a choice for yourself now and then (tea or coffee? Jam or honey? Walk or TV?) and see how the other person reacts to your decisiveness. Those few seconds to think and choose need to become a habit.

The difficulty might be that, when you think and feel the same way as someone else does, you feel safe for a while. But if that person then starts to think differently from you about something, this feels like a separation and will put you into a spin. This could make you subconsciously feel very alone. Someone not thinking, feeling and wanting the same things as you gives you a sense of being abandoned by them, which can leave you feeling bereft. The easiest way to take away this momentary, but horrific, sensation is to boot out anyone who doesn't think the way you do, anyone who doesn't make you feel connected to them through this merging of minds.

Graciousness is about knowing who you are in relation to another, that you are a separate being with points of connection. At the heart of this blue state of mind is the underlying belief that if one person exerts themselves as an individual, it must inevitably diminish another. It can lead to people diminishing another first, just in case.

Often the person with this blue marker will feel alone because, when they get close to someone, they begin to feel invaded or threatened and have to push them away again. Then this feels like abandonment by the other. So a potential lover says to you, 'Come for a drink.' You say, 'Yes,' and have a lovely time, feeling close to this person. They ask you out for a second date in three days' time, but you say, 'No,' because you actually feel rejected – the invite didn't come soon enough. In all genuineness, you tell your friends the person didn't ask you again, and the real invitation for the second date feels like abandonment.

EXPLORE:

- When a relationship is floundering, are you too clinical and quick to move on? Are you secretly proud of this ability?
- Do you deal with breakups in a way that is respectful/kind to your ex-partners?
- Do you take time to stop and think about your partner's point of view?

TIPS:

- Don't move on too quickly from relationships – take time to explore them.
- In order to develop a more compassionate view to balance your robust self-identity, take more time to observe and consider the consequences of your actions.
- Try to get into the habit of asking your friends how they are. Listen to the response. Get into the habit of putting yourself in their shoes.

Graciousness in the Family – Blue

You are gracious and capable in your decision-making, but you tend to overlook the effect of this on the others in the family unit. You at times lack empathy in understanding their troubles.

The parent with the blue marker here might encounter a lot more battles with teenagers, because they will often wish to intrude into a child's life (criticising their choice of friends, clothes, lifestyle, tattoos, piercings, eating habits, interests, university, etc.). Conversely, they may also push the child away if they feel their position is threatened in any way. In this case, it may well be because the parent is finding it hard to have a child who is separating and forging an identity that doesn't match their expectation.

EXPLORE:

- Do you ask family members how they are feeling? Or do you expect them to seek you out if there are problems?
- Can you make tough decisions with aging parents without being subsumed by worry?

Or,

- Do you get over-clinical in future decisions about people you love?

TIPS:

- Make proper time to find out how your children are feeling. Is there anything worrying them? Make sure you concentrate on their answers.
- Put yourself in another's shoes – try to visualise what could comfort or help them.
- Do you prevent yourself from getting overwhelmed by another's difficulties by becoming too detached? Be aware of that possibility.

Graciousness in the Workplace – Blue

Having a blue domain here may be advantageous in a position of authority. But you may tip into the tendency to press on in the belief that all is well, while actually leaving a trail of carnage behind. This behaviour will lose the goodwill of the team, who will stop engaging. Balancing this characteristic will make you a more considerate and successful leader.

People who feel secure are less pushed around, and are less likely to push others around. They are more able to make decisions about another, about themselves and about the whole group based on the objective of the task involved rather than on a power game.

So it might happen that, for example, a good, stable boss says to the team, 'We've all been asked to tighten up protocols because we are getting new investment, so we need to share objectives and how to meet them.' The person with blue in this domain constantly turns up to meetings without having met the agreed objectives, believing the request doesn't apply to them and that, anyway, the protocols are rubbish. They constantly walk into the professional arena telling everyone else they are mugs for kowtowing to the outrageous new rules, in the process humiliating them. They project their own historical humiliation onto others with the expectation that they themselves will be humiliated by the team. Eventually the good boss has to do something about the person who is behaving unprofessionally. In the mind of the employee, this is the expected humiliation, making the good boss the persecutor and the employee the victim. The good boss has been set up to fail.

It is worth watching out for whether you often end up in a space feeling either like a victim or a triumphant winner over another. It's a cycle that may be built on unresolved loss at an early age, a bumpy separation that can't be spoken about. This can link to a sense that no one is trustworthy except yourself and anyone who agrees with you. It can be closely linked to the rebellious blue domain, someone who can only feel separate if they push the other out of their head, rather than allowing them some space in their mind knowing it won't take over who they are in their own head.

EXPLORE:

- How often in your decision-making do you consider the feelings of others in the team?
- Are you always the one asked to make tough 'people' decisions?

Or,

- Do you secretly take pride in your ability to move people on or make them redundant without being unduly worried?

TIPS:

- Take time to imagine what the consequences might be and how other people might feel as a result of your decisions or actions.
- If you find making tough 'people' decisions difficult, look for a sounding board in someone else, so that you can look at situations through another's eyes.
- You may be cutting yourself off from your own emotional literacy. Notice that you might be perceived as ruthless. Consider whether your ruthless streak may hide anxieties and fears that you have long forgotten.

Adaptability

Do you find not sleeping in your own bed, in another's house, difficult? Do you hate being in an unfamiliar environment, or eating unfamiliar food? Do you carry your safe shell with you wherever you go, like a protective exoskeleton?

Or is your sense of self inside you, supporting you internally like a skeleton, carrying and protecting your heart and hearth? Are you able to tolerate unfamiliar surroundings and still return to the benign and stable home base? Can you take uprooting and living in any soil, not being anxious in others' spaces or a new company or moving home, accepting nutrients from elsewhere?

Try to imagine that a wild animal is heading towards you, and that, in fear for your life, you have to flee. Your heart is pounding away in your chest. It responds to the stress and exertion of the situation by beating more rapidly and forcefully. Once you reach safety, and stop to catch your breath, your heart will gradually return to its normal resting state.

Now, imagine the situation in someone who has previously had a heart attack. This type of event causes damage to the structure of the heart muscle, reducing its flexibility. The heart is less able to respond in the normal physiological manner, to rise to the challenge of a fight-or-flight situation. This person might end up succumbing to the physical danger.

It is similar with the subconscious. When the healthy mind finds itself in a situation of attack, it has evolved mechanisms to adapt to the situation and protect itself. If, however, the mind is less flexible than usual, because of unconscious stress from developmental stages, it might be unable to respond in a normal psychological manner. This less healthy mind might succumb to the mental stress.

The coding for this domain is all to do with response to anxiety and stress. The adaptable brain will flex to accommodate the stressful situation, and will continue to think and function in its usual manner. The inflexible brain finds it more difficult to flex, instead putting up a walled fortress inside itself to stop other things happening. It is like the immune system's response to trauma, when the immune system kicks in and up go the bruises, blisters and callouses. Someone with blue coding for this domain will feel many things as an attack – lots of little events and conversations, whether unpredictable and new, or based on known patterns from the past and wholly predictable in their mind.

The less adaptable your mind is to the external environment, the more likely you are to be very sensitive to comments by other people. The more sensitive you are, the more the world feels as if it's getting in your face, or dismissing you, and the more you have to defend yourself. The more you have to defend yourself, the more carefully the castle walls of your mind get constructed and the higher they go. The higher they are, the harder it is to come out from them and be in unfamiliar places. The more you need to control your environment around you to feel safe, the more likely you are to become stuck in an earlier developmental state of mind and the harder it becomes to recover back to a flexible and mature state of mind if you don't have your castle walls – or whatever has come to represent these (same food, same train, same boss) – around you.

Where adaptability comes from

When a child becomes panic-stricken, their parent picks them up. If they are not picked up and can't see their parent, the child will wander around in a panic. They stop thinking or looking and start behaving like a 'rabbit in the headlights'. Reasoned thought is no longer possible. Instead of stopping and thinking, 'Mummy must be near . . . I know she's near, she never leaves me . . . I'll just stop and think,' they become mentally paralysed and often move further and further away from their parent. When they find the parent again, they weep with relief and are tightly held. They can begin to function again. But children who have not had that response from an available adult do not learn to sidestep their panic sufficiently to be able to continue thinking clearly.

As we pass through this stage of infancy, and our capacity for rational thought increases, we learn to adapt to stressful situations. Where once we were paralysed by the fear of darkness at bedtime, we become able to soothe ourselves. We gradually accept from experience that we will wake up in the morning, and that someone will be there for us again. The monster under the bed is rationalised; the night lamp can be turned off. As we progress further, our internal world becomes secure enough that we can go out of the front door and walk to the shop, undertaking with ease what would once have been regarded as an impossibly terrifying expedition. Step by step, we learn that exposure to stress is followed by a return to our usual safe space. Crucial to this learning process is the reliable availability of our carer to scoop us up and reassure us that we are ok, before we wander off too far.

In this context, availability is not simply having someone's physical presence, but having someone else's entire focus when we are afraid and needing comfort. An adult may be physically present, but mentally distracted – for example, by other children needing attention, or issues at work. Their mind is elsewhere and therefore they are not wholly available for the frightened or anxious child. This doesn't mean that we will cause permanent psychological trauma if we occasionally respond to work emails at the same time as trying to listen to a synopsis of the latest playground politics. But in the extreme situation where an adult cannot be available for the child because of their own trauma (maybe injured, bereaved, grieving, worrying about financial difficulties), the child will find it harder to manage their own anxieties.

It doesn't need to be a parent who is available: older siblings, favourite teachers, extended family can all play the part. Many people can support the child through the process of adapting to 'difficult' situations. The child may experience a little angst, but they gradually learn to adjust to new or testing situations (first day of nursery, first sleepover with grandparents, first sleepover with friends, first day at school). They learn to think, 'Just as my parent puts their arms around me, I can internally put my arms around myself and give myself a hug until someone else comes along.' Self-soothing children can put up a bit of a wall when they need to, but with a little help the wall comes down again very easily because they know the difficult situation they were in was not an attack, it was a circumstance, and someone is there for them again.

In the event, however, of a lifetime of non-availability from adults, a child cannot learn to comfort itself: they have no role model. So they end up with a visceral dislike of change, a deep-rooted need to have the comfort of familiar objects and situations.

Changing circumstance is viewed as an attack, and they will erect fortress-like walls to keep it out. As adults, when something happens which requires them to be flexible in their thinking, it may trigger anxiety instead.

This person might become quite inflexible and intolerant, unable to adapt to certain situations because they are in defence mode. They cannot throw open their front doors and engage with difference and newness. Although this person can believe themselves to be very adaptable, they are actually very controlling of their environment – in that way, their mind is kept working and thinking. Some may even develop anxiety or panic attacks, or, at the other extreme, move into a self-sufficient space where they absolutely deny the existence of any anxiety or worry. The key point here is that their anxiety is shutting out any underlying feelings.

POINTS TO CONSIDER:

- Do you recall any instances of panic in your own childhood when you found yourself 'lost'? Is the recollection vivid? Can you recall what you were wearing? Can you envisage how the dynamic around events like this may have had long-lasting consequences on the way your mind developed?
- We tend as adults to assume that absence is understood as absence. We forget that in young children it may be perceived as loss. We think that because they go to nursery or school every day, they will realise that the separation is temporary. In fact, they might not. The younger they are, the more help they need. Their experience will create their perception of the world.
- It may be worth talking to young children about the difference between planned absence and abandonment.

For young children, there may be temper tantrums associated with getting out of the door to school in the morning. Try saying, 'I think you might miss me a bit today. I'll miss you too, but I'm thinking of you and I'll see you later.' Name the fear together, and reassure them that you will definitely be back home later.

• For small children, avoid the use of sanctions of adult company/absence as a form of discipline.

Adaptability in everyday life

The benefits of having an adaptable brain are apparent in all spheres of life. Historically, the greatest military and political leaders have been those with the ability to adjust to changing circumstances. Manufacturing industries respond to fluctuations in market demand by altering supply. The leaders of our technological industries in particular face a rapidly changing landscape.

Those with blue in this domain may have limited insight into this characteristic. They may regard themselves as being highly adaptable, when in reality the only moves being made are from one similar environment to another. Hydroponic plants are a good illustration of this. They are grown in a nutrient-rich solution and can be transplanted with ease anywhere in the world, as long as they remain in their nutrient jug. They cannot put down roots in soil. They are superficially adaptable, but only by taking their environment with them; they do not bed down in their new environment. This could be reflected in relationships (a string of similar girlfriends or boyfriends, for example), or in career choices (as with the travelling business executive in the example below). This person subconsciously manoeuvres their environment to prevent change, to keep themselves safe. OCD characteristics are an extreme representation of this need to control the environment in order to manage the anxiety.

Case Study: The Travelling Business Executive

Josh works in a senior position in a large multinational company. Over the years, he has been parachuted into various far-flung branches in order to troubleshoot. He prides himself on the speed with which he settles into his new environments. He regards his adaptability as a real asset to the company.

Josh was taken aback when his Cambridge Code report revealed a blue brain, and raised the 'error' with the Cambridge Code team. A bit of discussion revealed that, each time Josh was assigned to a 'new' position, he would actually be working on the same project, within the same management structure, in a similar format of office, and staying in a branch of the same hotel chain. Interestingly, on foreign family holidays, he chose also to stay in hotels from this same chain.

For the blue-domain person, issues may arise when the environment changes in an unpredictable and uncontrollable manner. Life events such as the birth of a child, marriage (even after perfectly happy cohabitation), divorce, moving house, etc. can impact significantly on wellbeing. Change, even when the trigger is a good one, may be perceived as risk. For such people, foreign holidays may not be the enjoyable interlude experienced by others.

Redundancy is often a particularly difficult situation. Even a person with green in this domain may struggle with redundancy: they may have to dig deep to find a way to keep themselves together, to keep moving forward. This can happen at any level, from their first paper-round to the established senior manager position. But, for those in the blue domain, redundancy may be catastrophic, triggering all the worry and anger responses. They collapse and cannot bring themselves to find a new job in case it happens again. The effects roll into their relationship with their partner, not just because of the likely financial difficulties, but because they subconsciously transfer to them all their deep-rooted anger at the unavailability of their childhood comforter.

At an earlier stage, changing schools can also challenge the adaptability characteristic. Is adaptability enhanced or restricted by being passed to-and-fro between the households of divorced parents, or between the dual environments of home and school? The answer seems to lie in the supportive availability of the adult/carer at both ends, rather than in the journeys themselves. There is often a short-lived kickback directed at the parent who is 'abandoning' them. 'I'm not going . . . I'm not taking that kit.' But this swiftly develops into familiar contentment at the other end. In schoolchildren, there is often travel anxiety associated with the journey to school, but delight when they arrive at the school they adore. Here, it is the journey which may be associated with the perception of abandonment rather than the school itself.

To flourish as a parent, try to be emotionally available to children, especially early on, when they need a greater sense of safety, and after an absence. Be patient; understand that there are a lot of things that to a child seem like unavailability. To a two-year-old, putting the baby sibling to bed can feel like an attack because, even momentarily and necessarily, the parent is absent.

Teenagers slamming a door in a parent's face are managing that space between wanting their parent to be available and unavailable – teenagers will manoeuvre their parent into being unavailable (so they can grow up), will feel abandoned as a result and slam the door to abandon the parent first. Teenagers, especially, are rollercoastering between physical availability and internal self-soothing as they learn to be separate. If the parent is also inflexible and feels under attack, their own default response can be triggered and they will slip down the developmental ladder and become childlike in their response.

If you code green for adaptability

You have a flexible approach to life's ups and downs – you are pragmatic rather than dogmatic. You have a balanced ability to adapt to changing circumstances, and are able to assess and respond to change in a reasoned manner. You accept it, and, indeed, sometimes actively pursue change.

Adaptability in Relationships – Green
Although you have no deep-rooted fear of change, be aware that there may be some upheavals that push you in this regard. Be aware too that your partner and friends' attitudes and reactions to change may be very different from your own.

For you, home is inside you, supporting you internally like a skeleton, carrying and protecting your heart and hearth. Don't be offended if some of your friends invite you round but don't seem to want to come back to yours, or don't want to visit your offices – it may be their insecurity, rather than a rejection of you. Don't underestimate yourself – this is an invisible but remarkable quality.

EXPLORE:

- Explore friendships and relationships with a broad spectrum of people.

- Enjoy finding it easy to adapt to your partner's family environment.
- How did you cope with your most recent house move? How did your partner cope? Who supported whom?

TIPS:

- Make the most of the fact that you are not 'thrown' by change and enjoy spending time with different types of people.
- Don't forget that the way you fear about certain situations might not be true the other way around.
- Be tolerant if your partner or friends are less adaptable. Your very secure inner self allows you to create a home wherever you go – others might need more familiarity.

Adaptability in the Family – Green

Your flexibility is generally an asset in the family setting. Your wellbeing and that of your family will thrive when you all do something different together.

EXPLORE:

- Are you the one who settles the family in when you are in a new place?
- Do you wish that your family would be more adventurous in their holiday destinations?
- Are there any members of the family who find change more unsettling than you?

TIPS:

- Accept that some routine is good for children and families. You can probably cope with or without routines but be aware that younger members may not yet have developed that adaptability.

- Fear of change tends to become stronger in later years. As you get older, try to maintain your flexible outlook. Keep ringing the changes.
- Are you sensitive to the anxieties of those who struggle with change? Remember some in the family might feel the loss of familiarity more than you.

Adaptability in the Workplace – Green

Your flexibility is likely to make you a valuable commodity in the workplace. It will be recognised that you can adapt to different tasks, different teams and different locations.

EXPLORE:

- Do you actively seek to challenge yourself?
- Do you think sufficiently about moving on/up/out in your career?
- Do you think about the security that your employees need? Do you support those who need to feel 'safer' during periods of upheaval?

TIPS:

- Actively seek out opportunities to work in different environments – you will enhance your skillset, your confidence and your CV.
- At different points in your career, explore whether you would enjoy changing sectors or even countries – you will thrive on the challenge of new circumstances.

- As a boss, learn to distinguish between true and apparent flexibility in your employees. Will their productivity thrive or suffer in an entirely new environment?

If you code blue for adaptability

You may find it difficult to adapt to a changing landscape, and it may cause you disproportionate distress. Subconsciously, you seek to control your environment in order to manage your anxiety levels. If you experience a rising sense of anxiety, it is important to seek support and share your worries before they escalate.

Remember that a subconscious desire to control your surroundings is not always a negative characteristic: it can be channelled into creating focus and energy, especially in those areas of life where your passions lie.

Adaptability in Your Relationships – Blue
It may be hard to accept that you have strong coding in this area, but self-recognition is the first stage to allowing your relationship and friendships to flourish. Fear of change will render you emotionally fragile when entering into or ending a relationship. It will be more stressful for you than for others. However, once you recognise that it is change that you fear, you may be able to move on more easily from an unenjoyable or damaging relationship.

If you find not sleeping in your own bed and being in another person's house difficult, and dislike being in an unfamiliar environment or eating unfamiliar food, be aware that it is not that the other person's bed or food is not good enough. It might be an insecurity or sense of being unsafe within you instead. Try not to criticise or diminish the space or offerings of others, which you probably do in your head, if not aloud. Try to imagine that their space or offering is good enough to be secure.

EXPLORE:

- How do you respond to the breakup of a relationship? With anxiety? With anger?
- Do you ever experience disproportionate anger when your partner or friend is unexpectedly absent, or even just a few minutes late?
- Do you and your partner or friends respond differently to change? Moving house? Arrival of a baby?

TIPS:

- Try not to stay in a relationship simply because you fear change. Push yourself to seek out a different type of person. Challenge yourself to explore new avenues in order to find them.
- Recognise and accept your difficulty with upheaval. Be gentle with yourself. Explain your feelings to your friends.
- Share your anxieties with your partner and enlist their support.

Case Study: Text Distress

MC was in a strong relationship and having fun with a great partner, JD. They had friends in common, were aligned on major issues and had recently moved in together. One evening, JD said he was meeting up with an old school friend after work but would be home no later than 7 p.m., in time for a takeaway and a film. MC sent some jokey texts to JD throughout the evening, but became increasingly twitchy when there was no response. At 19.07, MC texted, 'Where RU? U promised 2B home by now.' And another one at 19.12: 'RU ghosting me?' By the time JD wandered in at 19.20, a distraught MC fell on him with accusations of cruelty.

When MC later took The Cambridge Code, it transpired that she had a blue brain code for adaptability. Which explained why a twenty-minute 'abandonment' by JD tended to stir up the abandonment issues in her background.

Adaptability in the Family – Blue

As already emphasised, recognising that you may be blue in this domain may take a while. But perseverance may pay great dividends in the family setting. Your own self-understanding can lead to more empathy and patience in dealing with anxieties in other family members.

EXPLORE:

- Does your tendency to restrict your own horizons result in you restricting the choices of other family members?
- Do you feel your own wellbeing is compromised when close family members change direction? Do you always like to celebrate anniversaries in the same place?
- Are you making the best decisions for those around you or are your decisions based on fear of the unknown?

TIPS:

- For major upheavals, e.g. moving house or changing job, try to plan your support strategies ahead of time.

Communicate to your family your anxiety about being unable to control your environment.

- You may struggle to introduce variety into family activities, but managing your internal fears might make others happy.
- Try to touch base with your own emotional world; discuss feelings with your children and other family members – perhaps with their support you might find it easier to broach a new venture.

Adaptability in the Workplace – Blue

Remember, this characteristic is not a bad thing – it can be adapted very effectively if you own it and use it wisely. A certain dogmatism can be channelled towards working with real focus and energy, particularly for causes or professions about which you feel very strongly. It may be used as a strength, making you capable of longevity in a role.

However, if you want to change environments, move around, be seen to be adaptable, this inflexibility will have to be addressed. Be aware that you may have a habit of throwing up strong walls on a regular basis, and plan accordingly. Try not to shut people out but recognise that this may happen. Allow them back in, because that way lies growth and development.

EXPLORE:

- Does the suggestion of a 'new challenge' fill you with dread?
- Are you happy to work in a new environment, but only if it takes a similar form to the old one?
- Do you enjoy the 'sameness' of your job?

TIPS:

- If you are comfortable in your current work situation, relish it. Do not feel obliged to volunteer for a different role or a new environment without good reason.
- You will thrive with a constant and familiar team around you. If moving on or up, try to construct a familiar environment, maintain a similar routine, utilise similar systems.
- If you become aware of rising anxiety due to change, react early in seeking support from colleagues, a supportive boss or a professional counsellor.

Analytical

Do you analyse obsessively from every angle until you are paralysed with fear or anxiety? Do you check every possible scenario? Does everything in your house have a place, not just for tidiness but because you feel unsafe if things are left lying around? Do you get teased that you think things through too much?

Or do you find it easy to just get on with life?

This was a real conversation at the end of a dinner party:

Host: 'Would you like tea or coffee?'
Guest: 'I don't know. I might not get to sleep.'
Host: 'Have whatever you'd like. We've got herbal tea if you don't want caffeine. We've got ginger, fruit, green. What would you like?'
Guest: 'I don't know, whatever you think.'

The host is now in a difficult position. They have been told that caffeine will keep the guest awake and are forced into having to choose on behalf of the guest. If the host says, 'Ok, I'll get you a cup of green tea,' that then becomes an intrusion, taking away the agency of the guest, who might end up feeling resentful even though they said they would accommodate all the way. In this case, the host was too well mannered to make that decision and intrude, so an awkward pause ensued. The guest finally made a choice – fruit tea. The host left to make the fruit tea and, while they were out of the room, the guest turned to the dinner table and said, 'Oh no, I've given the host more work to make a special drink for me, and now I've completely offended them and what am I going to do?' For everyone else in the room, it created an 'eggshell moment'. The host had effectively been attacked by the guest with the suspicion that they might be such a monster as to mind the request. This situation arose because the guest over-analysed the choice and its possible consequences, in an unconscious effort to appease someone inside their own head.

Where analysis comes from

Over-analysis can arise out of poor internal scaffolding. For example, if a child is constantly called out by their parent on things, the child becomes wary of making a choice that might have bad consequences. The classic scenario is where a child visits a friend's house. The friend's parent offers strawberry or raspberry jam and the child's response is 'I don't mind' or 'I don't know'. The child wants to know what will make the other person happy. A child with strong scaffolding will respond, 'Thank you very much, I'd like strawberry jam.' But this child can't make a straight-off-the-bat decision such as: 'I like strawberry jam, so I'll have that, thank you.' Instead, they begin to analyse the offer: 'Will the strawberry jam give me the response I want from the person offering it to me, or will the raspberry jam give the desired response?' This is a tiny example of how over-analysis can start. In the instinct to appease, the brain becomes paralysed by this unanswerable question and cuts out: 'I don't know – you choose for me.'

As we saw in the introduction (see page 19), when a child is constantly questioned or undermined, their internal scaffolding does not develop robustly. They become increasingly wary of making a choice that might not be the 'correct' one. They begin to analyse every question in more detail. As the child carries their over-analytical brain into adulthood, their fragile internal scaffolding needs to be bolstered by some form of external scaffolding. This is provided by an obsessive analysis of the situation and those around them. There is a subconscious need to constantly check out and assess the situation, the other person, the potential outcomes, the prevailing wind-speed, etc. This characteristic often goes hand in hand with either compulsive tidiness or compulsive messiness.

Very analytical people often live in a world in which they know where everything is, but no one else can mess with their stuff – they are protecting it from attack. The more difficult and stressful life gets, the greater the inner turmoil and the more analytical this person becomes. They tightly manage their external world so that their internal chaos is held at bay. In its extreme form, someone with Obsessive Compulsive Disorder uses an excessive quantity and variety of external scaffolding (routines, rituals, totemic articles) to keep themselves propped up. Sometimes this constant analysis becomes so overwhelming that they shut down and appear detached or absent. The only way that they can continue to function is to shut out the emotional information overload.

Analysis in everyday life

In the workplace, there are distinct advantages to a strongly analytical brain, as evidenced by many senior managers and leading academics. Their minds are good at assessing possible moves and predicting the likely consequences, as in a chess game. People high up in an organisation will benefit from their ability to factor into the equation multiple different human and environmental factors before making a decision. There are, however, definite downsides. Decision-making becomes time-consuming. Questions can be so overthought that the mind becomes paralysed and unable to make a choice. The individual is rendered powerless and the decision has to be made by someone else.

POINTS TO CONSIDER:

- Don't be too quick to contradict the slow or simple decision-making of young children or inexperienced colleagues.
- If you are aware that you are analytical, try to understand where that comes from. Can you see that others may not be as upset by decisions you make as you have come to believe?
- Encourage vocalising your choices rather than believing over-politeness is helpful. It is more likely to be seen as exasperating. Watch out for when you do this.

In relationships, the analytical person may at first glance appear generous and accommodating. The response, 'I'll have what you're having,' suggests an easy-going nature. But in reality, this may be far from the case. This person's responses are really founded in fear – a fear of choosing 'incorrectly'. This is not a picture of healthy compromise, a conscious mutual accommodation which is truly generous, such as, 'Yes, I'll come for a walk with you today (even though I don't much like walking) because you sat and watched TV with me all day yesterday (even though you don't much like TV).'

This analytical accommodation of another person has evolved as a way of managing the risk of getting the answer wrong. This stress and hesitation can be baffling to the other person: they were genuinely just offering you a choice of two options!

In everyday life, the analyser can frustrate those around them because of the time they to take to mind-read and over-analyse before making a decision. 'Oh, just get on with it,' or, 'Just decide,' can be the constant refrain. Although some big life decisions require care and thought, it can be irritating for family and friends when even small decisions are analysed at length, from every angle. This can be especially hard for teenagers. When they ask, 'What time do I need to be back home?' they want a speedy answer, not an analysis of the pros and cons of 11 p.m. versus midnight. The teenager will rapidly turn to the faster-responding parent. However, some thought may also help them internalise the need for safety and it's that balance between the two that allows emotional wellbeing to flourish and emotional literacy to grow.

The analyser tends to be adept at manoeuvring. If they dare to make a decision, they might get it wrong. So instead they manoeuvre their sense of fear into a space where it is neatly and safely boxed. They are like a child who does not want to eat their breakfast, so they manoeuvre their food around the plate into a perfect pattern in a way that avoids them having to engage their mouth with the food. The analytical brain will assess and analyse and then manoeuvre those around them in the manner of a chess grandmaster. But their moves may be founded in fear rather than generosity or innovation, and this chess player may not always win the game, often leaving them bewildered and angry.

If you code green for analytical

You have a balanced sense of judgement and don't often feel the need to over-analyse your actions. You achieve a good balance between caution and trust. You are confident in stating your needs and wishes, and you expect others to be able to do likewise.

Analytical in Relationships – Green

You tend to rely on gut instinct combined with level-headed analysis in order to guide you in your relationship decisions. You are balanced between the 'heart' and the 'head'. There is indeed probably room for both. Remember to consider what your partner is: possibly head over heart.

Being green in this domain means that you have a healthy capacity to take in information, process it, make a decision and move on, because your internal scaffolding allows this to happen. You have not spent your whole life developing the antennae to assess the state of mind of another person in front of you in case something unexpected is coming at you.

EXPLORE:

- Although you are probably sufficiently cautious and safe in your use of dating apps, could you be more logical in your approach to relationships, rather than relying on gut feel?
- Are you generally healthily decisive around decisions with your partner?
- Are you sufficiently patient with friends who need to look at things from all sides?

TIPS:

- It never hurts to slow things down if you are unsure, though you are more likely to be safe than to take a positive risk.
- In an established friendship, accommodation of the other's wishes should be founded in generosity rather than analysis. Offer it. Expect it in return.
- Your analytical friends or partner are unlikely to change much. If you are in it for the long haul, you might need to find a way to tolerate this.

Analytical in the Family – Green

You find it easy just to get on with your family life. But be aware of the temptation to rush through things too quickly. You don't want to miss signs in others, especially the younger members of your family.

EXPLORE:

- Are you able to make decisions with some care but without over-thinking them?
- Is family life snakes and ladders or a game of chess?
- Are you sufficiently patient with other members of your family who take longer to come to a decision?

TIPS:

- Make a point of being patient with analytical family members.
- Debate your children's decisions rather than immediately overruling them.
- Remember to involve other stakeholders in family decisions. Appreciate that they may take more time to give their answer.

Analytical in the Workplace – Green

You have a healthy capacity to take in information, process it, make a decision and move on in a reasonable time-frame. Your decisiveness may be a valuable commodity in some jobs, but don't be afraid to take extra time or care in situations where the stakes may be higher.

EXPLORE:

- Do you tend to go with your 'gut feeling'? Are you usually correct?
- Do you pay due attention when a job involves detailed analysis of data?
- Do you take sufficient care in decisions that involve the money or health of others?

TIPS:

- Recognise your ability to make swift and confident decisions. Encourage others where necessary to 'take the bull by the horns'.
- You are balanced in your capacity to assess situations, but don't forget you may well need help for a job that involves detailed analysis of data.
- You may need to concentrate harder for the more multi-faceted tasks that involve detail and data.

If you code blue for analytical

You have a tendency to focus too much on details. You can be over-vigilant and over-keen to explore every option. You may not find big relationship decisions difficult but you do take your time over them and rarely rely on instinct. You will find it hard to act on anything like a 'gut instinct'.

It is common to lack insight into this characteristic and you may feel that this blue scoring is not 'you'. If so, take a moment to imagine a situation where many options are offered all at once. While grocery shopping, how long will it take you to pick out a cereal, or decide how much milk to buy?

People with this brain often oscillate between 'make this

decision for me' and 'how dare you even consider giving me advice!' Notice how many times a day you feel as though you have no power, and yet how many times a day you let someone else make a choice for you, either because you asked them to or because you couldn't say no. Try to make a choice when it is offered, however uncomfortable it makes you feel – don't set yourself up to be powerless. The desire to over-think things can lead you to leaving the final decision to another, but do be careful that you don't afterwards feel resentful that you didn't ultimately have a choice in the decision. It may in fact be that you have subconsciously set yourself up to be left out of the end outcome.

Analytical in Relationships – Blue

You have a tendency to over-analyse and are likely to appreciate this characteristic in others. You may feel uncomfortable if your partner or friends try to rush you into decisions.

The response 'I'll have what you're having' can look very generous, an accommodating way of managing life, but actually, underneath, there is a problem of fear. If you choose tea and you fear the other person secretly wanted you to choose coffee, then you fear their rage will fall upon you and push you out.

EXPLORE:

- Do you dither?
- Have you ever lost a potential soulmate through an inability to commit?
- Do you sometimes sense frustration in your friends at the length of time it takes you to reach your decision?

TIPS:

- It might be the moment to work out whether you are dithering because of a fear of getting it wrong.
- Realise that people who are genuinely offering choices want a genuine answer. Your mind may find this hard to accept, but it may be true.
- Do not treat your relationships and friendships like a game of chess. Try from time to time to trust your instincts and get in touch with your emotional inner world, rather than your analysis.

Analytical in the Family – Blue

Family members might occasionally be frustrated with the time it takes for you to arrive at a decision, because you consider all possible outcomes first, then default to 'you choose'. Their choice does not often make you happy, which does not make them happy. Your blue coding in this domain originates from your decisions being questioned and undermined in childhood. Remember that history tends to repeat itself.

This has given you a strong sense of caution, which can fruitfully be applied in the interests of your children's safety. But you may need to create a balance by introducing an element of fun and spontaneity.

It is difficult for children to experience constantly being attended to. They need to be kept in mind, to be understood, and they need a parent to be 'present'. Being either absentminded or constantly over-attentive to what they are thinking and doing can be equally unnerving for a child.

EXPLORE:

- Are you seen as the 'Health and Safety' parent? Do your children turn to the other parent for a speedy response?
- In wider family discussions, do others roll their eyes when you are mid-conversation?
- Do teenagers and their decision-making make you nervous?

TIPS:

- Beware of a tendency to over-analyse your family's reactions and responses. Try not to frustrate them with lengthy situational analyses.
- Bear in mind your fears might dampen spontaneity. Sometimes let another overrule your caution.
- Although it is good to be concerned, try to accept that youngsters often get to the same place a different way.

Analytical in the Workplace – Blue

The blue analytical domain is a mixed blessing. Although a little over-analysis makes for good leadership and judgement, too much can be paralysing. Although cautiousness can be put to good or even essential use, over-analysis can slow you down, irritate colleagues and prevent you from seeing the bigger picture.

The good thing about over-analysis – and, as mentioned above, many CEOs and academics have this – is that your mind can be put to analysing what the world might look like if things were moved around. People high up in an organisation often have a good dose of over-analysis because they need to be able to take into account multiple different factors based on the circumstances in order to make a decision. So the good side to the blue domain is the ability to make decisions based on that analytical formation. The bad side is when it gets to a point where you can't make that decision.

Case Study: Renting a Flat

Two friends decide to rent a flat together. They visit several potential options and sit down over dinner to discuss them. One of the friends immediately announces they had a 'gut feeling' preference on the walk-around. The other draws up a spread-sheet analysing the pros and cons. After several hours, the first is fed up and they decide to come back to the discussion the next day. And the day after. When they eventually phone the rental agency a few days later, the preferred flat is unavailable. 'It was snapped up,' they are told. 'It was by far the most popular.'

EXPLORE:

- Do you over-analyse what might happen before you make any decision?
- Do you see others wishing to move on faster in conversations and decisions?
- Do you lose the interest of potential customers/clients?

TIPS:

- You will be unwilling to reach conclusions until every eventuality has been explored. Be aware that this may slow your progress.
- Your over-analytical brain is extraordinarily useful – just be careful that it doesn't paralyse you.
- You may thrive in roles that require strategy or policy, but it wouldn't hurt to trust your instincts from time to time.

Entrepreneurial

Imagine that you are walking your dog in the countryside and return home to find your dog's fur covered with cockle-burs. Do you roll your eyes, turn for your dog-brush and begin grooming?

Now, imagine that you are driving home in the fog, peering anxiously through the windscreen. You are momentarily startled by the eyes of a cat sitting on a fence on the roadside. Nevertheless, you eventually manage to make it home safely. Do you give a sigh of relief and prepare a hot drink?

For most readers, the situational responses above would be the usual ones. However, others have responded to these situations by analysing the circumstances, realising the potential in them and developing globally marketed products. The examples above inspired the creation of Velcro and reflective catseyes.

Welcome to the world of the outlier, the left-field thinker: the entrepreneur.

Where entrepreneurial comes from

From infancy, we have within us a growing and expanding perception of where we sit in relation to everyone else. This perception, which can be called our 'unconscious family' (see page 17), does not necessarily reflect things exactly as they are, but rather how we, as children, perceive them. As we mature, we carry this 'unconscious family' into our other relationships and environments – we take it into our partnerships, to the school gate, our workplace. It is an inherent part of our understanding of the way everything in the world ticks.

Families have all sorts of dynamics within them and experiences are gathered by different children without anyone doing anything wrong; it is the nature of human interaction within groups. One experience can be of feeling small constantly, and the response to cope with it is by making ourselves feel bigger inside. That can be difficult with a peer group. If our mind perceives the world as actually out to make us feel small, and we feel powerless to stop it, we can become stuck in this shameful place. A great way to manage it is to have a say over our environment, and where better than working for ourselves?

The development of the entrepreneurial domain is all to do with our perception of our size. We all possess the capacity to be humiliated and the ability to overcome this. We all have a varying tendency to repeat this cycle and humiliate others in turn. The entrepreneurial domain is very sensitive to belittlement, and develops a determination never to be in a position in the future where we can be made to feel small in the same way. This characteristic can be seen within the family setting or in children in school; it can arise out of a feeling of having been bullied or belittled in some way. There is often an unconscious determination to be different, so as not to repeat the cycle. So, a child doesn't attempt to belittle smaller people in the same way, but rather to reduce bigger people to their own level, or smaller.

One of the most effective ways of doing this is simply to say, 'No!' This is an extremely powerful tactic often employed to great effect by the entrepreneurial teenager. He or she can reduce a very powerful adult to their own level by simply saying, 'No, I'm not getting in the car,' and sticking to their guns. Adults can negotiate, humiliate or cajole, but in the face of a simple but categorical 'No', the usual ways of managing authority are bypassed.

For the entrepreneur, it is very difficult for someone else to have something that they don't, which is why entrepreneurs do not like having bosses. They are often very non-envious people up front, but they have a secret pocket of envy which is much more difficult to manage than conscious envy – they may feel they have to look good and be responsible for all their employees and their own family. If the entrepreneur is their own boss, this can get enacted, but if they are in a hierarchy of junior role and seniority, where there is potential capacity for humiliation or belittlement, envy towards the 'boss' may rear its head.

The entrepreneur often revels in this aspect of their personality but has difficulty acknowledging any problems with low self-esteem or worries about being humiliated in front of others. Their subconscious mind has built an inner protective core where they determinedly love who they are. But when something happens to trigger that unworthiness – for example, a tricky workplace situation – their stubbornness may fall away and their lack of self-esteem may rise to the surface. At this point, there may be a tendency to diminish others. Having once been on the end of perceived humiliation, and for the most part having made sure that a similar situation is never recreated, the entrepreneur may feel worryingly out of control at this moment. Their inner core has been breached and they are precariously vulnerable to every criticism or tendency towards feeling small.

POINTS TO CONSIDER:

- Do you recall being belittled often as a child? Do you subscribe to the view that this might have made you who you are?
- Be sensitive to situations in which children or young colleagues may feel belittled. Monitor the level of 'banter' between older and younger members of the family or office.
- Remember to give praise when praise is due – as frequently as possible.

Entreprenurial in everyday life

While those with green in this domain tend to find their employment niche within an organisation or hierarchy, those with blue are usually drawn to roles of self-employment or freelance work – for example, taxi drivers, hairdressers, tradesmen, etc. You will see many strong blue-brain entrepreneurs running small businesses as well as founding tech companies, online retailers, challenger banks, cleaning companies, service agencies, etc.

Interestingly, many teachers are entrepreneurs, drawn to the autonomy of the classroom. Although someone else undoubtedly occupies the position of Head, there is a traditional perception that engagement with them can be minimal and the teacher is left as head of their own classroom. A similar phenomenon may be observed amongst the medical profession, where the entrepreneurial-spirited may now be less suited to a more closely managed work structure.

In a hierarchical work setting, however, those with a blue entrepreneurial brain may find it difficult to reach their goals. They may find working for another person to whom they can't say 'No' challenging, and can end up in a 'victim' space where they perceive their boss as the humiliator-in-chief who is always having a go. Alternatively, they may work extremely well for a boss whom they perceive to be protecting them and saying 'No' on their behalf, a boss whom they do not perceive as favouring or belittling them in the workplace. This is often when the organisation is in the early growth stages or has remained small.

In the former case, where the entrepreneur does not manage to find their workable space, they will usually move on to another company and may fall into the pattern of repeating this victim-like relationship with subsequent bosses. Being sensitive to any suspicion of humiliation, they may react badly to boss power games which might not affect other colleagues. The boss is being set up to be the person whom the entrepreneur fears. In what is truly a great waste of entrepreneurial spirit and capability, this person may end up feeling put down and undervalued. Some may end up taking sick leave, putting in a complaint, or litigating against the company. However, the truly entrepreneurial-spirited will move on, set up something else, build something new.

Couples who both code blue in the entrepreneurial domain may work exceedingly well together running the archetypal small family business. They develop and live out their separate roles independently: for example, one of them adopting the role of front-of-house persona and the other staying out of sight doing the 'grunt' work. This may work very satisfactorily for many years, but crunch time often comes when they expand their business model, and subconscious envy rears its head. So, for example, in a small decorating business, the front person with the excellent people skills acts as the face of the firm, negotiating with clients, organising appointments, dealing with payments. The hands-on decorator possesses the requisite manual skills required to carry out the job.

Initially, all works extremely well, but as the business expands, the hands-on decorator may become envious of the apparent attention focused on the front-of-house person. Or the front-of-house begins to covet the peaceful phone-free environment of the decorator. Thus, many family-like entrepreneurial small businesses work extraordinarily well as long as they continue to do what they do well, and resist the tendency to over-expand.

Those with blue brain coding here also often choose to be stay-at-home parents. Full-time parenthood is quite an entrepreneurial space where the parent can run their own show, being as inventive and creative as they choose. However, it is a well-recognised, emerging phenomenon that, later in life, when the children have left home, the blue-brain stay-at-home parent will set up a thriving small business. They thrive on generating ideas and inspiring those around them with their drive and tenacity.

Blue brain coding here can be associated with a highly creative energy, and there is often a desire to transform and improve an existing situation. At times this can verge on an obsessive need to make things happen and to get things done as quickly as possible. This can make the entrepreneur a tricky leader, who will only really flourish by working with people who also 'get it' and help translate ideas into goals and then into realities.

For entrepreneurial people, not being in control is terrifying. As long as they can control their environment, they don't feel humiliated or shamed. If that environmental control is taken away, that stubborn core they have created is much harder to maintain and they start to feel open to every offence or develop a sensitivity to feeling small.

If you code green for entrepreneurial

You have a solid sense of self-worth. You are not overly sensitive to criticism, nor unduly flattered by praise. You are not unduly troubled by being told what to do by others, and can choose when to accept advice or leadership. Your balanced sense of self-worth in this space allows you to present an even keel to the outside world in terms of your ambitions and motivations, and enhances your general wellbeing.

Entrepreneurial in Relationships – Green

You tend to bring the element of stability to your relationships. If you have a blue-brain partner or friend, you need to understand that they want at all costs to avoid feeling small and humiliated. The challenge is in presenting criticism to them constructively rather than choosing to avoid it altogether. If you have a green-brain partner or friend, there will be fewer episodes of conflict, but on the down side you may miss out on some of the fireworks.

EXPLORE:

- Are you happy to accept, or at least consider, criticism?
- Do you recognise that you yourself have healthy self-esteem?
- How easily do you think you can gauge the self-esteem of those around you?

TIPS:

- Be cautious in the manner in which you criticise. It may easily be construed as belittlement.
- Don't always feel the need to 'be the sensible one' in the household or the relationship.

- Don't be overly cautious in experimenting with different types of relationships and friendships.

Entrepreneurial in the Family – Green

As an infant, you were provided with an environment that bolstered your self-esteem. You will appreciate the importance of doing likewise for the youngsters in the household and will provide an atmosphere in which they will flourish. At the same time, you will be able to accept direction and support from parents and siblings, and will appreciate their support.

EXPLORE:

- Can you identify a particular episode as a child where you were made to feel very small?
- Are there any family members more vulnerable than others to belittlement? The youngest? The step-siblings?
- In your household, how easily does friendly banter tip into belittlement?

TIPS:

- Observe carefully for signs of bullying or belittlement at school.
- Remember that bullying may be more difficult to spot as children become older, and that cyber-bullying carries its own particular virulence.
- Grandparents often provide a well of praise and an absence of criticism. Allow your children to wallow in this.

Entrepreneurial in the Workplace – Green

You are a reliable and effective team player, performing well in clearly-defined roles. You respond well to feedback and are happy to accept advice and help. But your career could maybe progress further if you tapped into your entrepreneurial self and made more of opportunities to take responsibility for your own decisions, to seize the initiative, to change direction.

EXPLORE:

- Do you look forward to the morning/weekly team meeting?
- Do you lean on a supportive boss?
- Have you ever been advised you need to be more proactive in your role?

TIPS:

- Make a concerted effort to make your own decision, or take the initiative, at least once a day.
- Accept that a variety of jobs and experiences looks good on a CV – push yourself to apply for new jobs and promotions rather than resting happily in your comfort zone.
- Be fair and thoughtful in your feedback to your juniors, recognising that some find this difficult to accept.

If you code blue for entrepreneurial

You are a born entrepreneur who will flourish when driving things forward and providing the energy for others to do the same. To the outside world you appear feisty, confident and energised, but this may be underpinned at a deep level by a subconscious lack of self-esteem. You are unlikely to have insight into this. You may well exist very comfortably in your own space, with an inherently determined belief that you are happy where you are.

You are generally self-confident, charming and perceptive, with an ability to persuade and cajole others along the way. Be watchful, however, that, when triggered by difficult circumstances, you may have an unforeseen tendency to develop problems with jealousy and low self-worth.

Entrepreneurial in Relationships – Blue

In this domain, blue people often attract. In entrepreneurial romantic partnerships, when it is good, it is fantastically good, and it looks to the world as though you are the perfect working couple, in sync, with a beautiful fit and complementary skills. But when it goes wrong, there is conflict at every turn. So, after a breakup, sometimes we hear people say, 'Oh, my goodness, but you were such an amazing working couple, your skills were so complementary and you built such a beautiful home together.' These entrepreneurial couples often look perfect, but then there is disaster. One reason could be that neither partner is able to recognise their own jealousies or problems with self-worth. It is, however, likely that they recognise these in their partner. This may give rise to blame, but, equally, recognising and understanding these characteristics in the other may show them a path to finding a way out of their difficulties.

EXPLORE:

- Do you feel slighted or offended on a regular basis? How often are these feelings justified?
- Do you find yourself saying in an angry way, 'It sounds as though you don't trust me.'
- Do you enjoy being the one responsible for others? And being without a peer group who might judge you?

TIPS:

- When you feel offended or small, stop and consider for one minute whether this might have risen up from within you rather than having been imposed on you by another.
- Learn to accept that you can feel as small as anyone else at times, and that you have to learn to live with it.
- Any entrepreneur reading this will probably say, 'Rubbish!' So, if you are one of these, give it a chance, because of course that is why you can't get out of it – you cannot allow yourself at any cost to believe that you could ever, ever feel small. You have spent a lifetime denying it.

Case Study: Setting People Free – Not Everyone is an Entrepreneur

Entrepreneurs tend to have limited insight into the fact that not everyone around them is also an entrepreneur. In particular, family-run businesses tend to have, at the top, a strong entrepreneurial spirit who presumes that their children will be as highly motivated and driven to succeed in the business as they are.

There is a retailing firm that is still privately owned by the family who founded it. The matriarch of the business could not understand why her expansion plans, led by her son, were not progressing. Every other aspect of the business was flourishing and the market conditions were just right. The business owner had been an early advocate of The Cambridge Code, using it very effectively to spot up-and-coming talent in her lower ranks. She decided now to bring in The Cambridge Code to analyse the senior management team in the new wing of the business. What The Cambridge Code saw was a brilliant, capable and driven team, but with poor leadership. Her son, despite graduating at the top of an elite university and business school, was not a leader or business driver. His Cambridge Code profile clearly showed that, although he had many superb attributes, he was not an entrepreneur; he was deeply cautious about making decisions, he agonised over the people decision-making aspects of the business and strongly concealed his authentic self. He was a wonderful man with different qualities to his entrepreneur mother.

When presented with this profile, the son was empowered to take agency of his own future. He admitted to his mother that he actually disliked business and was only doing it out of a misplaced sense of loyalty to her. He actually wanted to be an academic. Fortunately, he is now thoroughly enjoying studying for a PhD. Equally fortunately, his mother has hired a successful non-family member to drive the expansion, and mother and son remain on excellent terms.

Entrepreneurial in the Family – Blue

You have the imagination and potential to create and manage a wonderful home environment. But be careful not to become dismissive or jealous of the differing role of a partner or other family member whose strength may be in another sphere. (See case study above).

This can get played out in a family when a child gets to teenage years and approaches a point where they might start to become an authority in some way. This authority is then diminished by the adult. In public, the parent will say that that child is better than anybody else, otherwise it reflects badly on them. A classic scenario is where the mother is quite diminishing of her daughter (or the father of his son) and everything they do is just a bit wrong, never quite right. Out in public, however, the child cannot be simply great in themselves, they have to be better than everyone else, because they are seen as an extension of the parent. This is a very difficult space for a child because in private they are humiliated and in public they are over-praised.

EXPLORE:

- Do you relish the challenges of creating a home?
- Are you the person who provides the drive and excitement within the family setting? Do you sometimes resent this role when you are over-stretched?
- Do you tend to diminish your teenage children as they approach a point where they might develop an authority?

TIPS:

- Give thought and respect to the differing roles that go into running a home and being part of a family.
- Guard against repeating the pattern of diminishing your own children.
- A lot of this is about succession planning – have you sat down and thought about what happens when your child is pushing on your door? What happens when your child has more information and knowledge and capacity than you do? Are you repeating the pattern of having been made to feel small and then making others feel small?

Entrepreneurial in the Workplace – Blue

You are self-sufficient and thrive without daily scrutiny of your work by another. Rather, you are strong on self-analysis of your performance and will push to improve it. You may find your niche in self-employment or in freelance work. However, you may be more challenged by working in an organisation, and need to be wary of recurrent or sequential conflict with your line manager. Your preference would be a hands-off boss, whom you trust to fight your corner if necessary.

You may well find yourself in a position of leadership, where you will need to take care that you temper your high expectations of others, especially when it comes to innovation and delivery. Your energy and drive to make things happen may sometimes create tensions in the organisation if you frequently pull it in changing directions. Entrepreneurs may find that, after a period of time, businesses need greater stability and a more measured approach. So they move on to a new challenge.

Entrepreneurs are usually not very good at having a 'growth mindset' – they can only do something when they believe it's their own idea. It is only with age that they realise: 'That was something offered to me by another person and I was not able to use it well.' There are many difficult children in schools who are on track to get excluded because they don't have a growth mindset. They don't believe that a bigger person, such as a teacher, can give them something good, they only think that the bigger person will humiliate them. But these children can ultimately use what is on offer, they just have to do it in their own time and in their own way. We often hear, 'Well, so long as he/she thinks it is their idea.' This can have wellbeing consequences because people aren't being honest – they have to feed stuff in a particular way for it to be accepted.

EXPLORE:

- Are you in regular conflict with your boss? Do you feel undermined and belittled?

- Do you find it difficult to accept ideas from other people, finding it easier to believe that they are belittling you rather than attempting to help?
- Are you sensitive to the way you criticise others, particularly the more junior, in the workplace?

TIPS:

- If you work for yourself, ensure that you seek out and accept sufficient external advice to keep the show on the road.
- If you are in regular conflict with your boss, you may need to work hard on accepting and tolerating criticism or correction without feeling unduly humiliated.
- Seek out and enjoy new and different challenges and avenues.
- When you are refusing help, just stop and think, 'Why am I denying myself the thing that might help?' You have to confront your own lack of trust and the reality that no one is perfect. All help is flawed, and one of the reasons you reject it is because accepting flawed help will put you in a humiliating space. Until you can tolerate that space, all help will disappoint you because it will always be just a bit flawed.
- Entrepreneurs have a good dose of self-sufficiency where they will watch out for themselves. The healthy space in the team is where everyone wants to be the best and everyone eggs each other on to be the best they can and to grow. So rivals are not killed or neutralised, but exceeded.

Boundaried

Consider what happens when you are walking along the pavement and you meet someone coming in the opposite direction. Do you always give way? Do you march on and never give way? Or do you sometimes give way, depending on the circumstances – for example, the weather, the time of the day or your mood?

Does it affect your decision whether the oncomer is a parent with a buggy or an elderly person with a walking frame?

This domain is all to do with our boundaries and our respect for the others who co-exist in our world. For some of us these boundaries are clearly and reasonably established. For others, the boundaries are more blurred and inconsistent.

Where boundaries come from

This domain relates to the idea that our unconscious brain is built rather like the framework of a house in which, metaphorically speaking, we live. This house is divided into different 'welcome' zones: there is a space outside your house on the road, where all the strangers are; there is a space which is garden, where you are happy to meet the postman; there is the hall, which you are happy for certain people to come into (for example, to pick up their children); there is the living room, into which you can invite people; there is the more intimate kitchen, into which you might invite family and close friends. Then, of course, there is the bedroom, into which you only invite those with whom you are intimate.

Our minds play out the way in which we understand our internal 'home'. This home is all about boundaries and how we recognise who is allowed in and who is not. In some people the boundaries are not clear, so that anyone is entitled to go into the whole of the house, no matter what, but then they get frightened and everyone has to be thrown out again.

Boundaries are about recognising how much we understand in our unconscious mind that we really are a separate person from another, and that, at the point of meeting another person, we both have a right to engage, or not. We both can ask for things and be told 'no' to things. Some people never learn to be wholly separate from their mother; they are never fully able to know that their mother, or any other person, exists in their own right, with their own boundaries. When pushed or provoked, their identification with the other person becomes so great that they think, if they are allowed into their bedroom, then the other person is allowed into their bedroom too. They don't know how to draw a distinction between themselves and the other.

As with many of the other domains, the structure of the mind for the boundaried domain becomes established early in life, during the processes of weaning and maternal separation. Smooth and gradual processes of maternal separation set the foundations for the development of healthy boundaries, in our relationships, our workplace and our family. However, the maternal weaning and separation processes may be more turbulent in the event of, for example, maternal illness, childhood hospitalisation, parental bereavement, displacement by another sibling, etc. As a result, deep-seated subconscious perception may take root. The mind develops with the belief that the other person in a relationship may take them over, that they will be forced to exist as a merged person rather than two separate entities. This is an uncomfortable underlying concern, and may manifest as anxiety and indecision over relationships, or in being a poor judge of others. In its most extreme form, there develops the subconscious belief that you have to eliminate the other, that this is the only way you can survive, as only one can exist.

So, returning to the pavement analogy, the blue-domain person will always give way to oncomers OR will never give way to oncomers. If they always give in, it is because they feel they do not have the right to put themselves first; they fear being seen; they have a propensity to shyness. If they never give in, even for an infirm pedestrian or parent with a buggy, it is because they fear being humiliated and diminished. They fear they will lose respect.

The green brain is able to make the decision based on the circumstances.

POINTS TO CONSIDER:

- Facilitate and encourage your children to understand being their own person, even from a young age. Encourage and support early attempts to take responsibility for their own actions, even as your role as a parent diminishes.
- Emphasise consistency and courtesy in relationships with others: siblings, playmates at nursery, teachers, relatives.
- As teenagers reach the age of sexual experimentation, discuss the need for social and legal responsibilities and boundaries.

Recognising boundaries in everyday life

Someone with green coding in this domain has reached a maturity in their separation. Their strong sense of self has been accompanied by a development of boundaries reflecting the appropriate rights of themselves and of others to exist. This goes hand-in-hand with the expectation and understanding that boundaries will be set by others. So, in the house analogy above, instead of there being a scenario of invaders v. invaded, there is a more balanced expectation that one person will knock and the other will invite in. Or perhaps not – the refusal to grant entry is taken as the prerogative of the person who owns the house. It is not taken as a threat, and negotiation might be possible.

Occasionally, the person with green in this domain will experience a trip, or 'fall', and open a door to the wrong person at the wrong time. Or they will misread the situation and barge inappropriately through a boundary into another's space. But, generally, the green domain is able to recover and renegotiate the appropriate space.

On the other hand, someone with blue in this domain has not fully separated in mind. In general terms they are still quite immature. They tend to spend some time a bit further down the developmental ladder, rather than just occasionally slipping down there. At any given time, even when unprovoked or 'untriggered', they may not feel wholly adult, carrying with them the tendency to feel small or ashamed. So, the blue-domain person may sometimes try to stay small and keep safe, even though this is humiliating. Or sometimes their brain may react by saying, 'I need to be bigger, or more powerful, or I will be destroyed,' and it pursues an aggressive stance in a relationship or encounter. Boundaries are inconsistent: there can be a tendency towards over-engagement or overfamiliar behaviour, mimicking patterns of behaviour sometimes seen in younger children. Or there can be a tendency to depersonalise, to try to render the other worthless.

Someone with blue in this domain may fail to realise that they are encroaching on another's space or diminishing the other person. In its extreme form, this can tip into sadism, where the person derives an enjoyment from their power to wipe out the other and to create pain. Paradoxically, it can also tip towards masochism, with the underlying belief that if one individual exerts itself, the other must inevitably be diminished. Another possible way in which extreme blue brain coding can manifest is through a tendency to agoraphobia and claustrophobia, either internally or manifested in how the person lives in the outside world. The absence of boundaries becomes terrifying, and a profound fear develops that they will act destructively towards the world, or that the world might act destructively towards them.

If you code green for boundaried

You exhibit appropriate and consistent boundaries towards other people, in both the personal and professional setting. You are perceived as having integrity, as being honest and reliable. You don't 'overstep the mark' and the relationships in your personal life and in the workplace benefit from this.

Boundaried in Relationships – Green
You are straightforward and respectful in your dealings with partners, friends and flatmates. As like domains tend to attract for this brain code, you will find yourself pulled in the direction of friends or partners who are similarly inclined. Together, you can

generally maintain or renegotiate relationships despite circumstantial changes.

EXPLORE:

- Is it acceptable to enter your flatmate's room when she is out?
- How likely are you to read your boyfriend's phone messages or emails? Would he read yours?
- Do you borrow your sister's clothes without asking? Do you make alterations to them?

TIPS:

- Make sure you establish clear rules and boundaries when flat sharing with friends.
- Consider dating someone a little 'edgier' – they will push your boundaries and there may be a lot of fun to be had.
- Be honest and explicit as soon as you feel your boundaries have been breached.

Boundaried in the Family – Green

You are clear in your own expectations and boundaries, but you will need to guide and educate children in developing theirs. You will need to establish and clarify the expected patterns of behaviour for others visiting your home.

EXPLORE:

- Does your home reverberate with sibling arguments about 'invasion' of rooms and 'borrowing' of property?
- How will you react when your teenager brings a partner home? Will you set boundaries?
- Will you set boundaries for visiting friends?

TIPS:

- Give unambiguous advice to your teenagers with regards to the importance of boundaries for both physical and social-media contact.
- If this is difficult, enlist the help of other relatives or family friends.
- It might be beneficial to explicitly address any house rules that you want to extend to guests in advance.

Boundaried in the Workplace – Green

You maintain professional boundaries in your workplace towards your colleagues and clients. You will find it easy to win the trust of others and in turn you are happy to entrust your colleagues with responsibilities. You will find that your suitability is recognised for roles that require an obvious and straightforward integrity.

EXPLORE:

- How much 'embellishment' is acceptable on a CV?
- Would you cover for a hungover colleague? How often?
- Is it acceptable to borrow from petty cash with the aim of visiting the ATM at lunchtime to replace the takings?

TIPS:

- You may be suitable for roles in which a high level of trust is required.
- Consider that there may be times when compassion for colleagues trumps the rule book.
- Do not be naive in assuming the honesty of others if the evidence points against it.

If you code blue for boundaried

It is likely that at times you find yourself getting close to overstepping boundaries with others. Do you sometimes 'sail too close to the wind' in your professional or relationship dealings? You may find that the inconsistencies in your behaviour or your tendency to overstep the mark will raise doubts about your integrity in the minds of friends and colleagues, resulting in the loss of their trust.

You generally have an openness to new challenges and relationships and have a daring nature. While this might carry appeal in some situations, you need to develop an understanding and respect for the need for boundaries in others. Your behaviour is likely to be deeply ingrained, and you may need help from others in unravelling the subconscious origins of your mistrust and in learning strategies for understanding and respecting boundaries.

Boundaried in Relationships – Blue

As with the green domain, the person with blue in this domain usually attracts partners with a similar code. When there is perfect alignment, when both believe in the same way forward, there may be an exciting and fulfilling relationship ahead. However, it is easy for one to become challenged by the other, either in terms of mind space or in physical terms (perhaps sexually). This can be a difficult and defining moment as to how much you believe you are entitled to, in terms of where your boundaries are in relation to another.

Unfortunately, it can often be the case that one becomes paralysed and the other wants to act quickly without due thought. Or a yo-yo situation may develop in which one person can over-identify with someone else and pull them in strongly, believing that their partner or friend has the same feelings; but then react just as strongly against that person because they feel threatened.

EXPLORE:

- Do you respect the wishes of your flatmates and friends with regards to privacy?
- When you are dating, do you take time to ask and establish boundaries at each stage?
- Do you think your partner and friends trust you? Should they? Is it important?

TIPS:

- Always take time to check and respond to cues about what behaviours are acceptable.
- With friends and flatmates, drawing up a list of rules may help.
- If you have commitment difficulties in relationships, it may be worth analysing the causes of this with a therapist or life coach. Taking the time to understand the cause of your subconscious mistrust may ultimately lead to more fulfilling relationships.

Boundaried in the Family – Blue

You may have poor insight into your erratic boundaries and will need to make a conscious effort to provide a secure boundary system for your developing children. Family dynamics and inter-actions may be difficult for you, especially as the family extends to incorporate new partners of children, in-laws, etc.

EXPLORE:

- Do you take a laissez-faire approach to teenagers experimenting with sex? Drugs? Physically dangerous hobbies?
- How do you feel about holding the family purse strings?
- Do your relatives know what is private and what can be shared?

TIPS:

- Accept that you have a role in educating your teenagers with regards to the importance of sexual boundaries. If you do not trust your voice in this capacity, enlist the help of another.
- Family transactions are important – navigate them with care.
- Stop and think at the closed bedroom door of family and guests (or, for that matter, cupboard doors – see text box for Insight into Intrusiveness).

Case Study: Insight into Intrusiveness

Isabella was settling into a flat with a new friend. She describes how, early on in the flatshare, she was taken aback to return home one day and find her laundry rescued from the drier and neatly folded in her bedroom. What was intended by the flatmate as an act of kindness was felt by Isabella as invasion of her privacy.

Boundaried in the Workplace – Blue
Your tendency to make the most of a situation could lead to mis-trust from your colleagues. In return, you may have a deep-rooted mistrust of them. You may choose to 'sail close to the wind' to set boundaries in order to achieve success, but be aware that this behaviour may bring you great stress.

EXPLORE:

- Has anyone ever accused you of harassing them when you think it's just a bit of fun? At the work Christmas night out?
- Can you identify any of your financial dealings as 'adventurous'? Do you consider this an asset in your job? Would others regard it as such?
- Would you trust your colleague with your pension? Would he trust you?

TIPS:

- Really take stock of your physical behaviour towards colleagues. Do you invade their physical space? Can you see that this may be frightening or humiliating?
- Try to understand that one person's 'wheeler-dealing' might be construed as another person's dishonesty.
- Realise how little disappointment one needs to experience in order to judge the behaviour of someone harshly.

Part Three | The Corporate Cambridge Code

As explained in the introduction, The Cambridge Code was initially developed for use in the corporate world, as a tool for personnel screening and team dynamics. This chapter looks a little more at the development of The Code in this corporate world and the expansion of its use into other spheres.

Why Do We Use Psychometric Tests?

There are many means of assessing the suitability of a candidate or employee for a particular job. A CV, for example, provides tangible and quantifiable evidence of experience, providing reassurance that someone can 'do the job'. Behaviour patterns can be assessed at interview: is the candidate friendly or cold? Engaging or distant? References can further contribute to the composite picture being built up. But there are less tangible characteristics that can contribute to the suitability or otherwise of someone for a job, too, and psychometric tests provide another tool in our arsenal.

Devised literally for 'measuring the mind', psychometric tests usually take the form of a multiple-choice questionnaire performed under a time constraint, and they introduce a more objective element to the assessment of a candidate. Unlike the situation with a face-to-face interviewer, or with an employer faced with trawling through a pile of CVs, the psychometric questionnaire cannot 'have had a bad morning and be feeling grumpy'. As well as removing the potential for observer bias, they are also designed to tap into more hidden aspects of a candidate, such as cognitive abilities, attitudes and personality traits.

Of the many psychometric tests in current use by recruitment panels, almost all are based on the psychology of the Five Factor Model (FFM) of behavioural traits, which has its roots in the work of the great psychologist Freud, in particular. These five fundamental factors are: openness to experience, conscientiousness, extraversion, agreeableness and neuroticism. Beneath each factor there is a whole range of other aligned factors, which exist on a binary scale and can provide multiple data points for analysis. For example, 'openness to experience' sits on a scale which runs from 'inventive/curious' to 'consistent/cautious' and includes emotion, curiosity and adventure. A complex grid of different layers and intersections can therefore be constructed as a data set, and can be measured and statistically analysed to provide proof of a candidate's validity and reliability. One of the most widely used examples is the Myers Briggs Type Index (MBTI), which allocates the candidate to one of sixteen particular personality types.

Why The Cambridge Code is Different

Other psychometric tests look at exhibited patterns of behaviour, focusing either on visible behaviour or self-reported behaviour, and are built on the foundations of behavioural psychology. They are measuring 'how' we behave the way we do, but not 'why'. The Cambridge Code questionnaire, with its unique combination of self-reporting and self-exploration, digs deeper than others, down to the subconscious drivers that underlie those behaviours. It assesses the 'why' rather than the 'how' of behavioural factors. It makes use of psychotherapeutic measurements (such as the trips on the ladder we talk about in the introduction, and exploring the subconscious mind) rather than psychological measurements.

Think about everything that you see when you first look at a tree – the colour of the leaves, the size and shape of the branches, the girth or curvature of the trunk. Essentially, you are seeing how the tree presents itself to the world. This is a little like the behaviours and actions of a person that can be seen by others. And it is this focus on observable behaviours that is the premise of most of the other psychometrics.

Now consider the reasons why the tree may look as it does. Why is it the tallest? Why the different-coloured leaves? Why would it be able to weather a storm? Much of this is down to factors that are not shown externally – the roots, the nutrients in the soil, the nature and depth of the soil itself. This is akin to our subconscious. It's the deep-seated stuff that can't be seen, that we are sometimes not even aware of, that shapes our thoughts and actions. And that will affect how we perform in our workplace.

Getting Statistical

Because The Cambridge Code assesses 'why' rather than 'how', it uses a different kind of statistical analysis to other psychometric tests. There are different kinds of statistical analyses available depending on what you are measuring and it is possible to describe two main types of data.

To understand the distinction in the types of data further, consider the following scenario: you are sitting in a court room and a judgement is being made as to whether or not a prisoner can be released early. In order to aid the decision, statistics will be used that have been taken from all sorts of public data – postcode, gender, race, education, health, genetic make-up, ethnicity). Because they are using parametric probability statistics based on the gathering of millions of data points, a normal distribution will be assumed. On this basis, it may be decided that this prisoner is unlikely to reoffend and they will be released. In this situation, the behavioural and other external measures used to analyse the prisoner work at a level of the 'how' of behaviour. However, because the situation encompasses human experience and emotions, history, events, interpretations and deep psychotherapeutic factors, the real risk is more difficult to quantify. A measurement of 'why' the prisoner might or might not reoffend will be more appropriate and will therefore produce a more valid picture of the complexity of the whole person. This is the strength of The Cambridge Code.

So why can't you cheat The Cambridge Code?

The Five Factor Model uses parametric analysis of data and assumes a normal distribution. In order to create such a normal distribution there must be a direct link between questions ('items') and the outcomes, which are aggregated from individual item responses. The Cambridge Code does *not* assume a normal distribution and depends on a non-parametric test construction. It is carefully designed with the freedom from single-item responses having to be aligned with certain outcomes: i.e., no single question codes a single outcome. Behind the scenes, the outcomes are pulled together from many different elements of a whole range of items, and it is therefore nearly impossible to cheat the test and try to get a predicted type of outcome.

How is The Cambridge Code Used in the Workplace?

Over recent years, The Cambridge Code corporate team has noticed an increasing number of enquiries relating specifically to the wellbeing and work–life balance of employees, rather than to the more overtly profit-related matters of team structure and ideal candidature. As a result, in addition to the original corporate version, the new, enhanced version of The Code presented in this book is now being increasingly used.

The wellbeing aspect of The Cambridge Code is not, however, limited to commercial companies. It has been introduced, for example, in initiatives across colleges and universities. This is in the context of reports of increasing mental-health issues and suicide rates amongst students, for whom the burdens of growing debt and employer expectations are taking a significant toll. As we have talked about in the brain domain chapters, we recognise the importance of allowing youngsters freedom to develop their independence and resilience. But, in the western world, emotional adolescence occurs at a later time, often during tertiary education and away from the relative safety net of the home environment. Any transition increases the vulnerability of people with wellbeing issues, and the move into higher education and away from home may be one of the biggest transitions of all. Institutions, as well as parents, need to support those who are vulnerable, without criticising or judging.

We have included some case reports from our files to

illustrate how The Cambridge Code can influence wellbeing in the workplace.

Case Study 1: Making the Move from Public to Private Sector

A government civil service department was looking at hiring a technical expert from the private sector. However, they had been having higher than expected attrition rates from posts at this level for the last couple of years. It seemed that they were able to spot good talent at interview and persuade candidates to make the move from the private sector into government departments, but they were not able to keep them in the post for more than a year. At exit interviews these people were saying that they had found the move into the public sector just too difficult. Although they had been forewarned about the differences in style and culture (including, incidentally, the fact that it would take longer to make things happen), they found it difficult to adjust and their frustrations led to them resigning from their posts.

This government department had neither the time nor the money to be able to use a psychologist as part of the interview process. Instead, they used The Cambridge Code to specifically flag up those with truly adaptable and resilient brains. As a result, their retention rates have significantly increased. They have also learned the valuable lesson that they need to engage more actively with potential candidates, and to be more transparent with their on-boarding processes.

Case Study 2: The Bank Leadership Team

A challenger bank asked our Cambridge Code corporate team to profile their leadership team. The Code reports showed that four of the directors had very strong competitiveness domain profiles. We discussed this with the CEO, as we thought they might represent a challenging team to manage, but he replied that he enjoyed their competitive spirit and as long as they never competed with him that was fine. He felt that the insight he had been given into the characteristics of his directors would allow him to deal with them effectively on a day-to-day basis. In particular, it alerted him to their reluctance to hire at the right level, and the need for him to coach them in hiring the most promising candidates.

A year later, the CEO came back to The Cambridge Code team to say that the senior leadership team was doing well but he now wanted to seek new advice. The bank was acquiring a small competitor in the market, and one of the rivalrous directors was being suggested as the MD of the new entity. The CEO knew the director's worth and supported him in the appointment, but the company they were acquiring was concerned by his 'feisty' reputation and not happy with the suggestion that he was to be their future leader. On the advice of The Cambridge Code team, this director was assigned to work with a coach specifically to understand what lay behind his competitive spirit and to train him to have agency over when and how he harnessed it. He developed insight into the fact that some people found it difficult to work alongside his overly competitive behaviour. By talking through this characteristic with the senior management of the new company and by tempering his management style, he ensured that everyone felt more comfortable making the appointment. He is now the successful MD of the new joint venture, which is flourishing.

Case Study 3: Is the Frontline Team Resilient Enough to Cope with the Challenges Ahead?

A large, multi-site UK retailer was going through a major transformation programme as they moved away from traditional in-store shopping to a more website-based service, with click-and-collect initiatives and digital customer acquisition. The management were keen to retain many of their loyal workforce and to upskill them where necessary, but were concerned that this might result in undue stress for some of their employees. Which of their employees had the capacity to adapt to changing circumstances without putting too much strain on either their work–life balance or their emotional wellbeing?

The Cambridge Code was used as a diagnostic tool early in the transformation programme. The results identified pockets of resistance to change in some unlikely groups of people. The company was able to provide workshops targeted at increasing resilience and helping people to tap into their own adaptability and graciousness. It was discovered that, in some of the least resilient workers, work–life balance had been significantly compromised by the requirement for extra hours just to 'keep afloat' and that sick leave for stress/anxiety had become an issue. For these more vulnerable workforce members, additional support measures (for example, safe havens, counselling) were put in place to guide them through the process.

Case Study 4: Student and Staff
Wellbeing at a UK University

This case concerns a UK university which underwent a meteoric rise up the league tables, leading to increased pressure on the academic and professional staff as well as on the students themselves. The council of the university wanted to make sure that they did all they could to avoid becoming yet another distressing statistic in the free fall of wellbeing amongst staff and students in higher education.

In a two-phase project, the final-year students were all offered the opportunity, at no cost to themselves, to take The Cambridge Code questionnaire and to receive their personalised wellbeing report. Our Cambridge Code team then ran some on-site workshops, inviting anyone with concerns to attend group sessions where specific topics were covered. The most popular areas for support were the resilience workshops and how to manage spiralling anxiety when in a crisis. The student feedback highlighted their positive feeling of empowerment through the exercise, and the importance to them of communicating together about wellbeing issues alongside the traditional individual counselling sessions on offer. For those individuals in whom wellbeing issues had previously been identified, the questionnaire allowed them to have more targeted conversations with their counsellors.

We were also aware that teachers and lecturers might find themselves under an increasing burden of heavier workloads, as well as pressure to perform and deliver ever higher ranks and statistics. So our client also invited the teaching staff at the university to take The Cambridge Code and to receive a wellbeing report. Seminars were arranged for a follow-up, whereby they could understand more about generic subconscious drivers of behaviours, followed by specific targeted workshops, including 'Taking Back the Initiative', 'Robustness Around Balancing Your Needs and the Needs of Your Students', 'Reconsidering Your Wellbeing Dashboard and Learning How to Keep it Steady', and 'How to Increase and Tap into Your Own Resilience'.

The feedback from the university was of a resounding success, for both phases of the project.

Other Feedback from Employers:

'We have benched The Cambridge Code against a well-known psychometric tool which took four hours and cost us $6,000 and we can only say that The Code was a more enjoyable experience. Not only did it accurately pick up on all the issues that the longer session had taken, it actually showed more.'

Director, Leading International Firm

'Of all the tests I have ever taken, The Cambridge Code is the most accurate, and that includes working full-time with a clinical psychologist.'

Leading HR Director

'It has made a real difference to how I work with certain members of my team. I had not even realised that there was such a thing as someone being "needy". Now I take the time to be encouraging and give more positive feedback – it costs me nothing and I can't tell you how much happier the team is.'

Small Business Owner

'We put our front-line executives through The Cambridge Code. They all had different profiles and interesting strengths. But they all had one thing in common – every single member of the team had a Gracious Green code. It clicked. It is a great environment to work in – everyone is considerate to a fault, but the department as a whole doesn't have enough bite.'

Director, Retail Bank

Conclusion

If you've reached this point in the proceedings, you will probably have completed the online questionnaire, received your brain results, digested the report and gone back to revisit some of the domain chapters that are more relevant to your profile.

So, what next? We hope that you take the opportunity to look closely at the twelve domains and how each, whether blue or green, might be functioning in your life. There may be areas where you feel the balance is right for you, but where, for a colleague or someone else close to you, their strengths or challenges in this area impact your behaviour.

As we said at the beginning, this book is not intended to offer a quick fix, but to help us to actively choose paths in our lives rather than simply to submit to them. Our subconscious has been shaped by events from even before we were old enough to feed ourselves, and we cannot change these formative events. We cannot rewrite history, but we can seek to understand it, and to use this knowledge to inform our future decisions and have greater agency over our actions.

One fundamental concept for us to carry through into our daily lives is an understanding of the manner in which we slip on the developmental ladder many times every day. While we may not be able to control the manner in which this happens – our subconscious will determine this – having read this book, we are now in a position to more clearly pinpoint the occasions on which it happens, to recognise the precipitants and to identify the levels to which we fall. This gives us agency to develop strategies necessary both for avoiding the slips and for hastening our recovery.

We may be able to develop specific self-help strategies: verbalising our way out of slips to babyhood; emerging from a toddler-squabble with our partner by understanding our sense of humiliation and owning it rather than passing it back and forth; or disengaging from rivalrous conflict with a colleague by recognising our behaviour as belonging to a teenager. Or we may be able to identify in more general terms the times when our recovery from these slips is less robust than usual, when our internal scaffolding is wobbly, and acknowledge we need to resource ourselves in a different way. Making visible all that is under our own swirling seas and becoming self-curious about the DNA of our own mind can be a hugely rewarding, lifelong way of thinking about who we are, where we come from and where we are going.

Occasionally our book may raise issues or concerns that you feel unable to address yourself. If this is the case, please remember that The Cambridge Code is not a substitute for real-life support. If you are in any way worried about your emotional or mental wellbeing, you should seek help from those around you as well as professional or medically trained people – for example, your GP, counsellor or psychotherapist.

Feedback

We always welcome feedback, so please feel free to share your opinions with us on Facebook, LinkedIn or Instagram. Other readers have shared with us 'penny-drop' moments, flashes of recognition or clarity, and we have included a selection of these below. Hopefully, though, by now you will have experienced your own.

Feedback from Individual Clients:

'This is so accurate my boyfriend assumed
I had spent hours with someone.'

(Yoga Teacher, 25)

'I thought only my partner would ever be able
to see that in me (and it took him 5 years)
and it has taken TCC 20 minutes.'

(Retail worker, 42)

'The reflection of my own self nearly moved me
to tears. To know that someone else could see this
and it is not "bad" has really given me the ability
to make healthier decisions.'

(Administrator, 25)

'I had been close to splitting up with my partner because I
felt he was hiding things from me and I was worried that

he didn't really trust me. After we both did TCC, I saw that he has a blue perfectionist domain and hates admitting mistakes. So he wasn't having an affair or planning on leaving me, he just couldn't bear the thought that I might tell him off or not think he was perfect. Now that I have met his mother, I know exactly why.'

(University Student, 23)

'I knew I was needy. I have now had the confidence to tell my boss. I wasn't embarrassed and told him it was because I also nurtured the team for him, so it was a positive. He said that he didn't always tell me when I had done great things in case I felt he was being condescending. There is now much better understanding all round.'

(Junior Office Worker, 19)

'I knew that I would be a blue code for the authentic domain. I think it's only professional to keep your private business to yourself at work. But when my girlfriend suffered a miscarriage I was very distracted, and I decided to break the mould and let my boss know. He was very supportive and I think now we probably both have increased respect for each other.'

(Bank Worker, 33)

Biographies

Dr Emma Loveridge, PhD (Cantab), MA (Psych), FRGS

The official bio:

Dr Loveridge is Founder and Director of Rafan House, a psychotherapeutic clinic in central London, where she works with a team of clinical experts. Her specialist areas of clinical work and research are the internal unconscious family and its manifestation in families and the corporate world. She is a member of the British Psychoanalytic Council (BPC). She is also Founder and Director of Harley Street Executive, which works with corporate boards and organisations, delivering both developmental coaching and clinical care.

The unofficial bio:

After her PhD in Theology and Philosophy at Cambridge, Dr Loveridge founded her first company: Wind, Sand & Stars. Her inspiration was the desert, its transformational effect on visitors and the partnership between east and west. She spent many years working in the desert with the Bedouin tribespeople, bringing trade to the area while respecting tribal life. Since returning full-time to the UK, she has spent many years in the field of family dynamics, health and wellbeing, including refugee families and child welfare.

Dr Curly Moloney, MA (Oxon) Physiological Sciences, MB BChir (Cantab)

The official bio:

Dr Moloney is a qualified Doctor of Medicine, obtaining degrees from both Oxford and Cambridge, where she was interested in conscious and subconscious brain activity. She afterwards joined the commercial world, founding the international executive search firm Moloney Search in 1994. The company works with corporations, governments and family offices across Europe, Africa and the Middle East, and counts over one third of the FTSE 100 as clients. She is a trusted advisor at board level across many organisations.

The unofficial bio:

At the age of twenty-six, Dr Moloney left her career in medicine without a backward glance, to set up her successful executive search business. She balances this with many charitable interests. Her own personal score for the 'rebellious' domain (see page 101) ranks amongst the top scores of many thousands of individuals tested to date. Although very little fazes her, it is with mounting horror that she realises that her own children have inherited her rebellious characteristics.

Although Drs Loveridge and Moloney may sound like unlikely partners, they have worked together since their time at Cambridge. For many years, and in many different locations, they scratched their heads over a new way of allowing people to understand their subconscious. They bring different perspectives to the project. For Dr Loveridge, the driver has very much been a desire to broaden understanding of mental health. For Dr Moloney, familiar with a variety of psychometric assessment tools in her businesses, the aim was a swifter, more insightful assessment.

So, in 2013, The Cambridge Code was born. With support from a team of Cambridge psychologists, the lengthy processes of scientific research and rigorous trialling began. And now, many thousands of people have used The Cambridge Code and benefited from its insights.

It is a source of great satisfaction to Dr Moloney that The Cambridge Code (TCC) has been taken up by business clients to aid insight into their people. Her TCC team assists clients in government and in the FTSE 250, working to align personnel with core employee characteristics. It is a source of great satisfaction to Dr Loveridge and her team that they have created a tool to facilitate access to and assessment of mental health and wellbeing.

For both of them, it is a source of even greater satisfaction that they have succeeded in their goal of providing you, the reader, with this new route to self-understanding. Hopefully this will bring to you a sense of 'coming home', a sense of acceptance of who you really are. Hopefully, too, it will also bring you the potential to make changes.